To David

AIMING
HIGH

Kind regards

Geoff

By

Geoff Lenthall

ISBN-13: 978-1517067038
ISBN-10: 1517067030

To my dear wife for her infinite patience for playing second fiddle to my computer.

CONTENTS

INTRODUCTION

Many books have been written by members of the Armed Forces, of their experiences during World War 2 and I have had the pleasure of reading many of them. They were true stories of bravery and sacrifice, excitement and humour and told with typical modesty by ordinary men subjected to the rigours and hardships of wartime service life. They were called up or volunteered to serve their country at an age when most of us today would be considering our futures and learning a trade or profession. My own personal interest was reading books by ex-RAF or Fleet Air Arm personnel who had taken part in operations over Germany or other theatres of war and survived to tell the tale. Stories of heroism beyond the call of duty told in a self-effacing manner of death and destruction, tragedy and heartbreak with the unbreakable bond of comradeship in times of adversity to survive.

This book is not about one who fought in the war, but someone who just missed out by virtue of age and circumstances, and reflects the thoughts and disappointments of one eager to join the RAF and train as a pilot. I volunteered at the minimum age of seventeen and a quarter, but was placed on the reserve until final call up in mid-1944, before the war ended. I served for nearly four years and met many ex-bomber pilots who had been fighting the enemy since the outbreak of war, and to me they were men to respect and admire. Some of them were Polish who had escaped from their homeland to join the RAF and I had the pleasure of flying with them on many occasions.

In addition to the recollections of my service life I have retraced my steps from my schooldays through to employment in the bank, working in the fishing industry and in publishing. Three very different ways of earning a living, which together with service in the RAF, widened my horizons and broadened my outlook on life.

***

Born with a plastic spoon in my mouth, I first saw the light of day in the mining village of Langold in Nottinghamshire in the year 1925. I cannot remember much of those early days except that I was told that my father worked as a window cleaner down the pit. So gullible was I that for some time I believed it to be true. At an early age the family moved to Brigg in Lincolnshire, where my father worked as a linotype operator with the local newspaper. A few years later he was transferred to Scunthorpe to take up a similar position with the Scunthorpe and Frodingham Star.

As I grew older my ambitions and aspirations fluctuated between excelling at school and going to Oxford or Cambridge University to obtain a degree, training to be a pilot in the RAF, becoming a professional footballer or Formula One racing driver, or even as a last resort, aiming to be a diplomat or Prime Minister of England. It's called spreading one's bets and I always was a dreamer. Such were my thoughts as I spent my early days at Henderson Avenue School and later at Scunthorpe Grammar School.

For some reason, things did not work out and the above mentioned aspirations became just a fantasy in my mind. Was this down to lack of confidence, an innocent naivety, or had I been aiming too high? Perhaps I should have sued the education authorities for failing in their duty to give me a well-balanced and rounded education to fit me for the career I wished to pursue. It is true that I played football for the school and gained my School Certificate as it was called in those days. The war put a stop to any plans of going to university and I had a brief spell in the Westminster Bank before I volunteered for the RAF. My dreams of becoming a pilot were dashed when I was told that my aptitude tests revealed an eyesight problem and I ended up as a Radio Operator flying in Avro Ansons and Vickers Wellingtons. Not for me the DFC and bar and fortunately not the VD and scar after seeing the horrific films shown to us in our early days in the RAF. Enough to put anyone off sexual relations for life! After demobilisation I rejoined the bank on a temporary basis which lasted 26 years – never made it to Manager, leaving as acting Chief Clerk (and that was only because the Chief Clerk was off work for some time with a medical problem). Spent a year or so in the fishing industry, travelling the country touting for new business before being appointed a director of the company. Life in the fishing industry was a totally different kettle of fish, as one might say. From a white collar cushy existence in the bank, I found myself learning the trade by going down to the fish market in the early hours with the chief buyer to find out what it was all about.

From fishing to publishing, when I joined Lincolnshire Life, the county magazine, as Advertisement Manager, subsequently taking over and becoming joint owner with my wife. The nearest I got to becoming a Formula One racing driver was as a motoring correspondent for the magazine, which gave me the opportunity to test-drive cars, both on the road and on the track. We sold the business in 1988 and I retired when I was 62 years old. By then I was too old and lacked the necessary verbal dexterity to become a diplomat or Prime Minister.

In this country there must be thousands of nonentities who had visions of fame and fortune, but never quite made it. Perhaps we are on the same wavelength and you are thinking "There but for the grace of God go I." Should you wish to hear more of the highs and lows, the sadness, romance and humour and unexpected pleasures and coincidences of this particular member, then read on. The following facts reflect my experiences in the RAF and life after demobilisation, my leisure pursuits, including visits to other countries, and hopefully my grandchildren will find it of some interest in later years. If it's explicit sex you are looking for, then you could be disappointed. Not that I am against it, far from it, but you will have to use your imagination when you come across my romantic encounters, such as they are. It's all in the mind! Remember, I was just a callow, innocent youth in those days. How different are the youngsters of today with the knowledge and experience that took me years to attain. It has often been said that nature should have worked in reverse; born with the wisdom of mature years. If only I had the awareness and vision that comes with maturity, in my youth. Life could have been so different.

1. EARLY DAYS

School days, at home, ATC

37, 38, 39... "Looks like another heavy raid tonight," said my brother, as we counted the apparently never-ending stream of nose-down Whitleys and four-engined Halifaxes, heavily laden with bombs and incendiaries, on their way to some unfortunate German city. This was part of our nightly routine and to a teenager it was a heady, exciting time as we watched the aircraft gaining height from their bases in Yorkshire and Lincolnshire, counting them out and if we were awake in the early hours, counting them in. More often than not, there were less returning as inevitably some had been shot down by enemy aircraft or flak. Some made it to their home base, others had to force land elsewhere. The unlucky ones either died in a blazing plane or bailed out, to land in enemy occupied Europe and finished up in a Prisoner of War camp, their flying days over until the end of the war.

In the days leading up to the declaration of war everyone was issued with an Anderson shelter for outside or a Morrison shelter for putting up in the house and usually used as a table. My brother Bill and I had great fun helping my father to dig the foundations for the shelter, putting it together and covering it with earth. One of the problems was flooding and we kept a stirrup pump handy for bailing out. For heating we used an oil stove and in due course installed electricity. Not the most comfortable of places to spend the night but we made the best of it. What a treat when the all clear sounded and we could return to our beds after a hot drink. We had the occasional raid and the air raid sirens prompted us to dash for the shelter in the garden. My father was an Air Raid Warden and as a Sector Leader, he received an early warning on the buzzer plugged into our mains socket. As soon as the buzzer went, it was all systems go. Dad shot off on his bicycle to report to the local area HQ, whilst we hurriedly got dressed in warm clothing and made for the shelter. From time to time he would look in to see if we were alright and tell us what was going on.

A lot of the action took place in Grimsby and Hull and we could always tell when there was a heavy raid on Hull, by a huge red glow in the sky. Considering the fact that Scunthorpe was the home of two vast steelworks, the Luftwaffe only made the occasional sporadic attacks. On one occasion a Heinkel 111 was shot down and crashed near the Appleby Frodingham steelworks. This was a moment of excitement for most lads of my age and we cycled down to examine the wreckage.

Due to the petrol shortage during the war, the local bus company, Enterprise and Silver Dawn, equipped their vehicles to run on a gas mixture and it was odd to see the huge gasbags strapped on top of the buses, often driven by a woman. Private car drivers were limited to a meagre ration of fuel, that is unless they were in a position to obtain 'black market' coupons. The same applied to food and clothing and gradually all the wrought iron gates were dismantled and taken away for melting down to help in the manufacture of weapons of war. All windows had to be blacked out and sellotaped over in the event of an air raid. Motorists were compelled to place special covers over their headlights, which made it very difficult to see the road and obstacles ahead. Such were the complications of living a far from normal life in war time. Not only that, but there appeared to be queues everywhere – it was a way of life in those dark days.

My early school days were at Henderson Avenue School and we lived in Ashby, on the outskirts of town. This meant a two mile or so cycle ride and I distinctly remember my old headmaster W.E. Ramsden cycling to school along the same route. If we were early we would take great delight in overtaking him with a quick "Good morning Sir," as he appeared to have a problem. His cycle seemed to be permanently stuck in low gear (these were the days of the old Sturmey-Archer gears) and he appeared to be pedalling furiously and getting nowhere fast. Nowadays of course, even a lot of the pupils have cars or motor bikes and the thought of seeing one's headmaster on a bike is unbelievable. As headmasters were in those days, he was held in awe and respect and heaven help you if you committed a misdemeanour. It was many years later that I met up with him again when he was President of the Lincolnshire Lawn Tennis Association. I had been invited to present prizes at a tennis tournament in Lincoln and my wife and I were introduced to him. He was charming and as was typical of all good heads, he remembered me and it was a nostalgic meeting. I was tempted to ask him if he had sold his cycle, but thought better of it. During our conversation I was amazed at how many names of pupils he could remember.

My interests at this time in addition to the Air Training Corps, playing football and cricket, were making flying models of aircraft, from special kits of balsa wood and tissue treated with dope to tighten and strengthen the surfaces. To this day I can still recall the addictive smell of the dope. When completed, we took them to the nearby fields, wound up the propellers fitted with a strong elastic band and proudly sent them aloft.

I was also involved with a school friend, John Urry, in constructing a homemade three valve radio set and remember quite clearly hearing through the headphones my first radio contact, which was a broadcast of a song called 'Ama Pola'. What a thrill! Although sharing my excitement, my mother and father seemed more concerned with the fact that I was littering up the dining table with all the paraphernalia required to put it together, including the old accumulator and high tension battery. Not to mention the outside aerial attached to a pole at the bottom of the garden and brought in through a bedroom window.

I spent a lot of my leisure time at the home of my cousins about a mile away. My uncle was editor of the Scunthorpe and Frodingham Star and lived in Old Brumby where he had built a 'playhouse' for his children. We spent many happy hours making aircraft, playing with trains on a large track and generally getting into mischief, stealing apples etc. from the neighbours. Bob, the eldest eventually joined the Marines, young Dave went to work with his father as a reporter on the newspaper and Joan, who was interested with her mother in Amateur Dramatics, joined the local dramatic society. She was ambitious and eventually reached the top of her tree as a professional actress, appearing on television and performing on stage. She later married Laurence Olivier and in due course became Lady Olivier. I have only seen her once since she achieved fame, when I was in London and she was appearing in a play. I called in at the theatre and was allowed to visit her in her dressing room prior to her performance. It had been many years since we had seen each other and we had a lot to talk about, though time was limited as she was due on stage. My one and only link to the famous!

Bob finished up as a music teacher at the Royal Academy and Dave became a sports reporter and eventually landed the job of Managing Director of Granada Television in Manchester. Now that is what I call achievement.

I left Henderson Avenue school to carry on my education at the local grammar school, which involved kitting out in school uniform of green blazers and caps and for some obscure reason I still have my old school cap tucked away in a drawer. The school motto 'Be Strong' is still visible, but needless to say it doesn't fit. I can honestly say that my school days were happy, in spite of being caned by the Headmaster Mr. Taylor (quaintly nicknamed 'Sprut'), for being involved in breaking a window during a scuffle with a fellow pupil. I learned a painful lesson.

Most of the subjects I could cope with, but I could not raise any enthusiasm for English Literature or History, the latter being taught by Miss Wintersgill (nicknamed 'Fanny') if my memory serves me right. Chemistry by 'Faf' Hawkins was always enjoyable if only to learn the secret of making 'stink bombs' – unofficially of course. English Language and Maths were two subjects which had to be passed to gain the School Certificate and fortunately the Maths teacher, Mr. Glick, feared and respected, was a strict disciplinarian as well as an excellent teacher. Sports facilities were very good and I always looked forward to Gymnastics, Football, Cricket and Cross Country running. In addition to normal subjects, we were encouraged to grow potatoes and other vegetables in the school allotment as our contribution to the war effort. Posters for 'Dig for Victory' could be seen everywhere.

In those days the classes were graded into A, B and C and I was in B form throughout my days, so obviously there was no improvement in my scholastic abilities. It could be said that I was consistently mediocre. In 1941 I was successful in passing my University of Cambridge Local Examinations. History and English Literature were two of my least favourite subjects, but surprisingly I managed a credit in History, only by last minute swotting. English Lit was a dismal failure, as was Physics. I scraped through with a pass in English Language and credits were obtained in Chemistry, Mathematics, French and German. When I look back I realise that the subjects in which I was successful were taught by teachers with whom I had a good rapport and were firm in discipline. I enjoyed German under the strict eye of 'Bert' Benton, who had this odd way of punishing those who were not paying attention. He would take the board duster, rub out items on the blackboard until it was well and truly 'chalked', then wander down the aisle, stop at the offender and gently pat his head, leaving the embarrassed pupil with a chalk-covered head. Not painful, but another lesson learned.

Before I owned a cycle I used to travel to school on the bus and sit on the back seat with two girls, Peggy Maw and Gwen Long, who lived nearby. (Strange how one can remember names, yet my short term memory leaves a lot to be desired.) They were attractive girls but in those days I was painfully shy and found making conversation difficult. How I envied the lads who were confident and had no such problems. This failing on my part continued throughout my lifetime until maturity in later life. To possess the art of conversation is a wonderful gift and the mere thought of having to meet people was a nightmare. Even worse, the thought of having to give a speech of any kind filled me with dismay. In the whole of my life so far I can only remember addressing a gathering of people on three occasions and one of those was at our Golden Wedding celebration. Another occasion was when I was asked to give a talk at my local Rotary Club when one of the members went to sleep. It must have been a fascinating talk! One thing is for sure and that is one of my original bizarre ambitions to be Prime Minister would not have come to fruition.

At the time I was living in Scunthorpe and in common with a lot of my school friends, joined the Air Training Corps and couldn't wait for my calling up papers. Even though I wrote to the RAF Recruiting Office pleading domestic problems or any pitiful excuse to expedite my call-up, there was no response and I had to wait impatiently for the great day. They were busy days and nights as we were taught the rudiments of navigation, aircraft recognition, principles of flight, Morse code and the mysteries of the internal combustion engine. Nor were we spared the agonies of strenuous keep-fit lessons and 'square bashing'. I eventually reached the dizzy heights of the rank of sergeant and one of the things I enjoyed was taking continuity drill, when after the initial order to commence, it was all done strictly by numbers and timing. We were thrilled to visit nearby airfields including Kirton Lindsey, where the Americans were flying Lockheed

Lightnings, and Waddington, where we had the privilege of meeting Squadron Leader Nettleton, of Augsburg fame.

Neil Huntley, a friend of mine who was also in the ATC, thought that we should aim at getting ourselves fit prior to joining up. Good idea, I thought, so summer and winter saw us getting up 6.30am to go for a run around the fields near our home. It was on the bitterly cold wintry mornings that I began to wonder whether it was such a good idea, but we stuck it out and felt that we were physically fit for when the call came in the official envelope from the RAF.

Our commanding officer was Flight Lieutenant Whitaker, a strict disciplinarian but fair, and under his guidance we developed into a well-trained and efficient squadron (119). He was very popular, particularly when each year he would invite several of the N.C.Os to his house for a Christmas party. There were generous helpings of food and drink and one of the highlights to us was the competition for eating the most of any specified item of food. I fancied my chances but was usually out-eaten by one of my greedier friends.

Strangely enough, although there was no shortage of attractive girls around, not many of us seemed interested as there was but one thought in our minds and that was to join the RAF and do our bit. I was friendly with a girl called Isobel, the sister of Vic Wells, a friend of mine in the ATC and we saw each other quite regularly, though we both knew that the war would put a stop to any lasting romance. Apart from that, my mind was concentrated on learning as much as I could to prepare for entry into the RAF, and girls became a secondary consideration, for a while anyway.

By this time we were all in our first jobs after leaving school and just marking time. What spare time we had was taken up in social activities and I was persuaded to join the Campbell School of Dancing where we were to learn the basics of the waltz and foxtrot, before venturing into the intricacies of the tango and other exotic dances. I had already seen some of my friends being taught in the school hall during the lunch break and thought what a lot of sissies they were. Little did I think that I would be following suit later on. Although I found it embarrassing, I was told that it was one of the social graces and would stand me in good stead in later life. They were right, even though my terpsichorean skills were limited to the waltz and a version of the slow foxtrot. It was however, an excellent way of meeting members of the fair sex.

My brother had also been in the ATC and his ambition had been the same as mine, to train as pilot, but he likewise had an eyesight problem and qualified eventually as a wireless operator. He was two years older than I was and had already left and gone to Radio School at RAF Madley, near Hereford. I eventually followed him and was able to take advantage of his contacts in Hereford.

I remember Dad was quite a keen gardener and specialised in growing chrysanthemums. He did his best to get my brother and I interested but to us it was a passing phase and our interests lay elsewhere. Each year the garden would be a glorious show of colour, of which he was justly proud. Even to this day I can admire a beautiful garden, but somehow lack the interest to take part in its development. The thought in my mind was that it would be something to look forward to in retirement.

In his spare time Dad used to help out at the 'Old Show Ground' where Scunthorpe United used to play. At half time my brother Bill and I would join him in the Supporters Club and during the winter months we always looked forward to our drink of hot peppermint cordial. It would cheer us up if the 'Iron' were not doing too well. Frequent cries of "Up the Iron!" or "Up the Nuts!" echoed round the ground to encourage the lads.

My mother was also a keen gardener and an excellent cook. She had to be, to feed three ever hungry males. In those days, not only did we have three meals a day, but also supper, which quite often was a 'fry up' of leftovers. So in spite of rationing, we were well fed. I can remember on Pancake Day, sitting there knocking back several pancakes whilst Mum was slaving over a hot stove. And they were made with the aid of powdered egg from packets, but I loved them!

2. WESTMINSTER BANK

My first job

As I was only 14 years old when war was declared, any decisions as to a future career were not top priority as I knew I should eventually be joining the RAF. I was shortly to take my School Certificate examinations when I was approached by my uncle, who was a great friend of the manager of the Westminster Bank in Scunthorpe. In the course of conversation he had been told that there was a vacancy in the bank for a junior and thought I may be interested. It's not what you know, it's who you know! So, with nothing to lose, I applied for the job for which the possession of the School Certificate was essential. I started straight away on condition that I passed my exams and was given time off to take them. Fortunately I was successful, thinking at least it's a job with pay (little though it was) and it would keep me going until call-up time

Banking in those days was quite different from modern computerised banking. For one thing the staff were all male, though this was to change as all fit men were gradually called upon to serve their country. There were no computers and all entries were made by hand in massive ledgers. It was a delight to see all the account names at the top of each page written in beautiful copper plate handwriting. My job was to do all the menial tasks, such as making tea for the staff (a very important job), taking the post, buying stamps, and learning how to operate the adding machines. In addition I had to answer the telephone and keep the fire burning – woe betide me if I let it go out. In winter it was freezing cold as the fire heated two or three antiquated radiators, which threw out very little heat. Like so many other people I used to think that banking was a cushy job, with civilized hours of ten to three. Of course this was only half the story as we started at 8.45 and usually finished around 5pm, or even later if the cashiers couldn't balance their tills. The manager, usually the figurehead, by virtue of his position, arrived just before we opened and left around four, usually for a game of golf or similar recreation. Socialising in the club house was a recognised way of attracting new business and he was pretty good at it. In those days all the staff, apart from the manager, cycled to work and we left our bikes in the back yard of the bank, which was on the main street.

In the winter, the tiled floors were very treacherous as customers entered with snow on their boots. I well remember one of our farmer customers went full length on the floor and on picking himself up, said in typical broad Lincolnshire dialect, "Hells bells, that the'er floor is as sla'ape as snot." These days, he would have sued the bank for a bruised backside!

The running of the bank fell on the capable shoulders of the first clerk. He was a quiet, efficient man, married to a French lady with a young son and I got on well with him. Even more so when he took me into his confidence one day and when all the others had gone home, he took me into the manager's room and opened one of the large cupboards. I couldn't believe my eyes when I saw what to me was Aladdin's cave. All the shelves were full of chocolates, sweets, cigars, cigarettes, boxes of biscuits, bottles of sherry and whisky and other delicious mouth-watering provisions. It was and I believe still is, traditionally one of the manager's perks to receive gifts from grateful customers with overdrafts for looking after them. The goods on show were obviously over and above the rations allowed and it had been noticed that one of our customers who had an overdraft and owned a confectionery shop, was a regular visitor to the manager's room each week. My eyes were shining as I gazed open-mouthed at the vast array of goodies and Bill, the first clerk said that his lad would be pleased to have some and that no doubt I would not say no. He was right of course, so we each took a few of what we wanted and rearranged the rest of the stock. Later, the manager told Bill that someone had been at his sweet cupboard and blamed the cleaner, who lived above the premises. However, nothing more was said, as he knew that he was committing an offence by accepting black-market goods. So we breathed again and have had guilty consciences ever since.

As time progressed, I eventually graduated to the position of cashier, which was more interesting as it gave you the opportunity to get to know the customers. On the odd occasions when the till didn't balance, everything had to be checked back with batch and control sheets and 'meat tickets.' I never did find out why they were so called, but they represented all the actual cash received during the day. Naturally the search for errors resulted in a late finish and you wouldn't be very popular as all the staff assisted in locating the error.

One of the few perks in the bank, was the low interest rate on staff advances, which at that time was two and a half per cent. Another welcome diversion was the opportunity to visit Doncaster for the St. Leger races. Our duties were to man the change boxes by the Silver Ring entrance, exchanging money for the general public to gain admittance. We were supplied with a drink and a supply of sandwiches and when we closed down just before the races began, we had our lunch and had free admittance to the elite area. This involvement was done on a voluntary basis and there was never a shortage of those wanting what was in effect a pleasant day at the races.

All bank employees were encouraged to study for the Institute of Bankers examination and when the Bank Inspectors made their periodic visits, we were all interviewed individually. The subject of the examinations was always discussed and although it was not compulsory to take them, the Inspectors made it quite clear that you would be unlikely to make progress in the banking world if you didn't achieve your AIB (Associate of the Institute of Bankers). Even though you could take one subject per year, I was unsuccessful in passing all the subjects and this was possibly the reason why I did not reach the dizzy heights of Manager.

There were only six on the staff and one by one they were called up, until the great day that I had been waiting for arrived. I had volunteered as soon as I was seventeen and a quarter but was put on deferred service until I was eighteen and after aptitude tests at the RAF centre in Doncaster, I was eventually told to report to the Air Crew Reception Centre in St. John's Wood in London.

3. AIR CREW RECEPTION CENTRE

Joining up in London and moving to Torquay

On the first of July 1944, having said farewell to my family and friends, I packed a case and caught the train for Kings Cross. This was my first visit to the capital and it was with some trepidation that I boarded the train. It was pretty full, mainly of service men and I felt that some of them were probably wondering why I wasn't in uniform. During a conversation with a corporal in the Lincolnshire Regiment, I was happy to ease my conscience and inform him that I was on my way to join the RAF. Strangely, he seemed a lot more friendly towards me after that. That's how it was in those days; if you were old enough to enlist in the Forces and weren't in uniform, you would get some odd looks and were viewed with some suspicion.

Gradually the train started slowing down and I looked out of the window at the bomb-damaged houses, for London had been at the receiving end of heavy raids for some time. As the train drew into the station, I heard the familiar wailing of the air raid siren and the explosions of shells bursting from the anti-aircraft guns surrounding the capital. The station at Kings Cross was packed with hundreds of people, mainly servicemen and I made my way to the Tube station to find the train for St. John's Wood. As I hurried down the steps, I heard the first of many explosions as the German bombers found their indiscriminate targets. When I reached my destination, the air raid was still on and I was advised by a warden to remain in the station until the all clear. Half an hour later I was reporting to the reception area of the ACRC, where I was directed to my billet, which was in a converted block of luxury flats in nearby Avenue Close. It was here that I had my first touch of war at close quarters when a flying bomb demolished a block of flats in the next street and we were ordered to assist the rescue squad to bring out any casualties. Sadly, there were only three as the rest of the occupants were killed instantly. It was my first experience of the horrors of war and it was a sobering experience as we toiled amongst the debris, looking for survivors. Fire watching was one of the duties assigned to us on a rota system and we had to go up to the roof and keep a lookout for flying bombs, known as 'doodle bugs.' As soon as we spotted one and the engine stopped, we blew a whistle and ran like hell to the basement, hoping to get there in time.

ACRC 1944

After the usual kitting out and further medicals, we had to suffer the humiliation of the well-known 'cough test' and examination of our private parts, and painful inoculations when some of the lads passed out after the injection of the needle. Real training commenced in earnest and I settled down into service life with my fellow men from all walks of life. By this time the Germans had perfected the Doodle Bug (V1) and later the deadly V2 which gave no warning of its approach, and were sending them over to the capital in ever increasing numbers. Whilst marching from the billets to Lords Cricket ground for training, it was usual to wear battle dress, carrying a respirator and steel helmet and as soon as a doodle bug was spotted and its engine stopped, it was recommended to fall flat on the ground, helmet on head and hope for the best.

The RAF had taken over buildings near the cricket ground which were used for training and used as a canteen. On occasions when we were on fire-watching duty, we had temporary beds which were in fact trestle tables with mattresses. We soon found out the reason for this as when we climbed off the tables and stepped on the floor, there was a crunching sound as we crushed the many cockroaches which frequented the building. The visits of the Luftwaffe became increasingly frequent, causing further casualties, and the powers that be decided to evacuate from the capital to a more peaceful setting in Torquay on the south coast.

It was a mammoth operation and more by luck than good judgement, everyone arrived there and quickly settled into the various hotels which the RAF had requisitioned. It was a much more peaceful existence in Devon and Hitler only occasionally deemed it worthy of a visit from his bombers. I thrived on the marching along the promenade, PT on the beach and swimming in the sea, and began to think that life wasn't so bad after all, but of course it was early days and it wasn't all going to be as enjoyable as this. We were all comparatively fit young men and eager to learn but in the evenings we were able to enjoy a hectic social life when time permitted. No doubt most of us were away from home for the first time but there was no time for homesickness.

For most of the budding aviators it was the beginning of a big adventure and after a few weeks we were on the move again, this time heading north to another seaside resort, Bridlington. This was the location of the Initial Training Wing, the next step on the ladder to eventually reach our goal and achieve our ambitions to fly.

4. INITIAL TRAINING WING

Bridlington

During aptitude tests I had been told that my visual judgment was not up to the standard for training as a pilot, so I opted to train as a Wireless Operator. So much for my dreams of becoming a pilot. My next course was at ITW in Bridlington, where I spent eight weeks' rigorous training. We were billeted in hotels commandeered by the RAF and marched each day to the Spa for lectures, interspersed with PT, swimming and assault courses. We were up at the crack of dawn for breakfast, not quite up to the standard of that which was normally served in the type of hotel in which we were staying, but nourishing and acceptable. PT was not too popular for some and in spite of roll calls, there were usually one or two who had managed to skive off. The assault course, though strenuous and difficult, proved to be surprisingly popular.

Dinghy drill took place in the harbour and I looked down in horror from the harbour wall to the sea some twenty feet below. With Mae West securely fastened, we were ordered to jump into the grey water below. Holding my nose and closing my eyes, I leapt into the water, seemingly going down and down for ever, before surfacing with lungs bursting. We then had to swim to the bomber dinghy floating some twenty yards away. That wasn't so bad, it was the climbing in the dinghy that was the difficult part. Dinghy training invariably attracted visitors who came along to watch the fun, which wasn't welcomed by those who refused to jump and were subsequently taken off aircrew training by reason of LMF (Lack of Moral Fibre). This must have been a shattering experience for those involved who were re-mustered to ground duties and I thank my lucky stars that I wasn't one of them.

Situated on the east coast in a popular seaside resort, entertainment and dancing was on tap and we were able to enjoy a social life in our time off in the evenings and weekends. Surely it wouldn't be much longer before we started our radio course, but sadly there was a delay in aircrew training and I was posted to Blackpool, from one seaside resort to another, from East coast to West coast. Could have been worse, a posting to some isolated outpost in the middle of nowhere.

Blackpool was where I was to take a course on driving at the Motor Transport School and I was beginning to think that I should never see the inside of an aircraft, let alone fly in one.

5. MISEMPLOYMENT

Learning to drive at Blackpool

Blackpool was the home of No. 1 Motor Transport School where we were to train as MT drivers. This change in plan was quaintly known as temporary misemployment and once again we were billeted in hotels. I thought that it wasn't such a bad life after all and decided to make the best of it and enjoy life to the full. Here it was that I learnt the mysteries of the internal combustion engine, daily inspections, and the rules of the road. It wasn't so bad when we were let loose on the road in a saloon car, but when we graduated to Fordson 20 cwt trucks and the ancient Albion ambulances with crash gear boxes, it really tested our knowledge and aptitude to the full.

Four weeks in Blackpool, enjoying the amusements on the Pleasure Beach in my spare time and visiting the local dance halls, was icing on the cake for me. It was with regret that I heard, once again, that we were on the move, when the powers-that-be decided in their wisdom, to move the MT School down to Melksham in faraway Wiltshire. It was here that I graduated to heavier vehicles, including the articulated Queen Mary, used for the transport of aircraft. Eventually the day arrived for the passing out test, in which I was successful in gaining my RAF licence to drive. When I eventually returned to civilian life all I had to do was forward my RAF licence to the authorities and my civilian licence was returned. So in fact I have never taken a driving test in civvy street. At least I had learned one trade which would be useful in later life, even though I was no nearer to flying. It had been an interesting and practical course and hadn't cost me a penny! There were celebrations in nearby Trowbridge where we sampled the local brew until closing time before saying farewell to our comrades in arms who would be going their separate ways.

There were still no signs of recall to aircrew training and I was not happy when I was posted to Inverness transit camp for two days before making the journey to Sango, an isolated radar station located on the extreme north west tip of Scotland. Life was pretty bleak in this Godforsaken camp, relieved only by the occasional game of football on the cliff tops overlooking the North Sea and trips to the nearby mountains for rock climbing experience. One of the highlights was the appearance of a captured German submarine in Loch Eriboll, a short distance away. In such an isolated place there was not a lot of driving to do apart from the occasional 50 mile trip for provisions and spare parts. Otherwise it was a pretty boring existence apart from the odd date with one of the WAAFs, but the location was so remote and desolate, that there was very little entertainment apart from the camp cinema. I soon tired of this existence and became impatient for some real action, as the war was in its final stages.

6. THE EMERALD ISLE

Driving in Ireland

Still no signs of aircrew training, as my next posting was to Northern Ireland as MT driver. Although I had volunteered for overseas service on completing my MT course, I hadn't contemplated that Ireland would be considered as overseas. My destination was Ballydonaghy, another radar station near Strabane, in County Tyrone. It was a nightmare journey in a blacked out ship on the rough Irish Sea from Liverpool to Belfast, before taking the train to Strabane with John, a fellow driver from the London area.

Radar crew at Ballydonaghy

Together with Ken, a trained engineer, we were responsible for the transporting of the radar personnel to and from Strabane to the radar site, some 15 miles away near the border of Northern Ireland and Eire, by the river Liffey. All the personnel, some 20 in all, were billeted with local Irish families and John and I were fortunate enough to be staying with the Docherty family, mother, father, and two daughters. To me, this was an ideal situation and my thoughts and ambitions to carry on with aircrew training were pushed to the background. My letters home became less frequent as I sampled the delights of living in civvy billets without the normal restraints of RAF service life. No parades, no drill, no inspections, no Station Warrant Officer to bark orders – in fact I was in seventh heaven, particularly as the home-cooked meals were excellent and the ratio of eligible women to men was around eight to one at that time.

The radar shift consisted of eight men under a Canadian Sergeant, accompanied by a Corporal SP who maintained strict security with the help of his fierce-looking Alsatian dog.

The SP was not a particularly popular man and any opportunity to 'take the mickey' out of him was welcomed. There was mutual dislike between he and I, as I took great pleasure in driving erratically to upset him and there was one particular junction on the main road where the surface camber was very pronounced and when taken at speed, the ancient Fordson truck would rock and sway like a mad thing, much to the annoyance of the SP, who would shout at me and threaten me with jankers. Meanwhile, in the back of the truck, the radar operators were aware of my little trick and would cheer heartily when the truck nearly took off.

The radar station was located a short distance from the River Liffey and from time to time, weird noises were heard at night of animals splashing through the water and voices urging them on. I found out later that it was common practice to bring stolen cattle over the river from Eire to Northern Ireland, where they were sold for a profit, no questions asked. My curiosity was aroused by these incidents and John and I decided to take a trip over the border to nearby Lifford, a small market town. On visiting the shops, we were surprised to see the well-stocked shelves of food, clothing and other items in short supply in strictly rationed England. We made frequent trips, smuggling shirts, suits and many other goods which were difficult to come by back home. We never seemed to have any problems with the laid-back border guards.

After a few weeks, we had both settled down into a routine and John had become very friendly with an Irish waitress in a cafe we used to visit in our off-duty time. He was a dark, good-looking young man with a smooth, confident manner and Bridget was a friendly, attractive girl with a delightful Irish brogue. It soon became apparent that the friendship was developing into something much deeper and John confided to me that they were talking about getting engaged. I tried to talk him out of it, saying it was early days, the war was still on, and that he may have a problem with the religious beliefs of Bridget, who was a staunch Catholic. John was a lukewarm Protestant and said he was prepared to change his religion to marry her.

Meanwhile, being at a loose end when John was getting his feet under the table, I went to the local dance hall and met a vivacious blonde. Her name was Bernadette and she left me in no doubt that she wanted to get to know me better. This suited me, as I was reserved by nature and was of a somewhat retiring disposition, and found it difficult to get to know people, particularly girls. In fact she did most of the talking, which I welcomed. Our friendship blossomed and I was invited round to meet her parents, a friendly couple who seemed delighted to welcome a British serviceman into their home. Detta, as she was known to her friends, was a fast worker and knew what she wanted, and it wasn't long before we were making the most of the situation when her parents had gone out. Both John and I would spend many hours discussing relationships, religion and the future with Jan and Donna, the two daughters of our hosts, until the early hours. Strangely enough, apart from friendship, there were no relationships apart from a little innocent flirting with the girls, even though they were both attractive. Could have been something to do with their strict father, who had strong, fixed ideas about how young servicemen away from home should behave! He was a fair-minded fatherly figure and his wife was a wonderful cook, and with two lovely daughters under the same roof, what better arrangement could there have been? Many RAF personnel would have given their eye-teeth to have been in a similar position. But what about the war? Hadn't I joined the RAF to fight the enemy? My ambition was to become a member of aircrew rather than having a cushy time in Ireland, driving lorries and chatting up the local girls. I knew that it wouldn't last and sure enough, my posting came through to report to the transit camp at Manchester.

7. MANCHESTER

In transit

This was only a short stay in the temporary holding unit for RAF personnel in transit to new postings. We were based in Manchester, and I was able to contact Detta, who had already left Ireland to seek a job in England. She was employed as an au pair at the home of a doctor on the outskirts of Manchester and I was able to visit her and resume our friendship, which was getting deeper. Talk of engagement was concerning me as I felt that the future was too uncertain and expressed my feelings to Detta, who accepted the situation and asked if we could still be friends. I felt very guilty but with the war still on, I could see no point in getting seriously involved.

With two of my friends, I went to the NAAFI club in Manchester, where we discussed our personal problems over a few beers, before eyeing up the girls on the dance floor. Feeling merry and talkative after a few drinks, I surprised myself by asking one of the girls for a dance. I had spotted her earlier dancing with a tall, dark RAF sergeant and was immediately attracted by her auburn hair and friendly blue eyes. As we danced, I learned that she was training to be a teleprinter operator and was hoping for a posting near her home in London. Her parents were Irish and although she had lived in England for several years, she still possessed a delightful Irish brogue. Her name was Pamela, known to her friends as 'Paddy' and I had the odd feeling that I had known her for a long time, such was the rapport between us. As the evening ended, we drifted out on to a balcony, looking out over the city in the bright moonlight. I knew that I just had to see her again and we exchanged names and addresses and promised to keep in touch. Not being a man of the world and still feeling shy in the company of girls, I asked her if I could kiss her. She didn't say a word but just put her arms around me and lifted her face to mine. We held each other closely and I kissed her tenderly on her lips. This was the first of many and eventually we had to leave to catch the transport back to our stations. I was in seventh heaven and told my friends that I must be in love or something. They told me in no uncertain terms that it was a load of nonsense and that it was pure infatuation and the effects of the booze. They pulled my leg unmercifully on the way back, but I was unperturbed and just sat there with a smile on my face and my thoughts on the events of the evening. We made the most of our short stay and met again before my posting came through and we departed, promising to keep in touch.

8. CRANWELL

ITW Refresher course

My service life and movements seemed endless and I was beginning to think that I should never see the inside of an aircraft, let alone fly in one. Sure enough, it wasn't long before my posting came through to go an ITW Refresher course at Cranwell in Lincolnshire, less than 50 miles from my home. This lasted four weeks, during which I was able to take weekend leave and see my parents and friends. I couldn't believe my luck when I found out that Paddy had also been posted to Cranwell as a Teleprinter Operator and we were delighted to renew our relationship. We spent many happy hours at the NAAFI Club in Sleaford as well as exploring the Lincolnshire countryside and the local pubs. I knew that my next posting was due soon and once again I said a fond farewell to Paddy, wondering when we would see each other again. (Little did I know that some 30 or so years in the future, I should be at Cranwell again with my wife for the celebration of the Battle of Britain cocktail party.)

After the refresher course, during which I had been subjected to more square bashing, learning about hygiene, the elements of flight and navigation and the Morse code, I was eager to get to Radio School, but it was not to be. I could not conceal my disappointment when I heard that my next posting was to Kirton Lindsey.

Fortunately this posting was only of short duration, where I was to be employed in the Pay Accounts section, until aircrew training was resumed. By this time the war was nearly over and the demand for aircrew had diminished, so it looked as though my ambitions to fly operationally were not to be. I was naturally disappointed but consoled myself that at least I would be one of the lucky ones to survive the war. So I reluctantly learned about Officers' Allowances and similar boring account procedures until the day came when I was told that at last I was going to No.4 Radio School at Madley, near Hereford. I was over the moon and we had an appropriate celebration at the local village pub.

9. MADLEY

No. 4 Radio School – at last

Arriving at Hereford station by train, I was picked up with several others by transport and after a rough seven mile journey to Madley, found ourselves in a bleak, isolated camp, comprising several sets of Nissen huts spread over a large area by the airfield. So this was No. 4 Radio School – not quite what I expected. After the usual formalities I was allocated to my billet, a Nissen hut situated with several others in a wooded area. There were twelve beds with a roaring wood-burning stove in the middle of the hut. This was to be home for the duration of the course. Not quite the Ritz but cosy enough with the fire going full blast, and well out of the way of nosy SWOs and their like. Trouble was that it was well out of the way of everything, including the ablutions, which were about a mile away. Daily routine involved getting up and dressing and marching with packs on backs to the ablutions, washing and shaving, then marching another mile to the dining hall for breakfast. Then on to the Administration Centre for the first lecture. On such a dispersed camp, marching from place to place was the order of the day and in wet weather, and there was an abundance of that, regulation issue capes were worn. It was a wet and miserable place with living conditions on the primitive side, particularly when compared with the life of Reilly we had in Northern Ireland.

As well as learning the intricacies of the TR1154 and 1155 radio transmitter and receiver, I was surprised to find myself one day lobbing hand-grenades at targets in nearby woodlands. I never did discover the significance of these exercises, but it was quite exciting, particularly when one of the lads pulled out the pin and inadvertently dropped the grenade in the bunker. Fortunately the sergeant in charge was quick off the mark and picked it up and threw it out of harm's way. All in a day's work for him.

One of the perks available to the cadets was working in their off-duty time at the nearby Hartley's jam factory, loading jars of jam into packing cases. Not only did they get paid, but some of the more daring ones were known to smuggle out jars in their battle dress. I was one of the unlucky ones when one of the jars escaped from my person and smashed on the road by the exit gate. Needless to say, I was banned from the factory.

Day after day, I was immersed in transmitting procedure, fault-finding and building up my speed on the Morse key. It was not surprising that one or two of my friends developed a version of the *Doolally Tap*, or *Morse Madness* after lengthy sessions with headphones, sending and receiving at speeds of up to twenty-two words per minute. The unfortunate ones were taken off the course and posted away for re-mustering on other duties.

The day eventually dawned when we had our first flight in a De Havilland Dominie, a military version of the Rapide, an aircraft specially converted with five radio sets for air instruction. They were twin-engine biplanes and were also used for communication duties throughout the war. After initial training on the Dominie we graduated to the Percival Proctor, a military version of the Vega Gull, a low-wing single-engine monoplane. This was a much lighter aircraft and more susceptible to the effects of strong winds, and some of the lads found that they were prone to air-sickness and were taken off the course.

In the Proctor, apart from the pilot, there was a somewhat cramped position for the radio operator and it was here that I learned about loop bearings, dead reckoning positions, and not forgetting to wind in the trailing aerial! Another thing I always remembered was the call sign of RAF Madley, which was 7D7. It is strange how one can remember things that happened years ago, but short-term memory tends to be virtually non-existent. It was obviously the air training that I enjoyed most, when we became proficient in frequency changing, back tuning, diversions and homings and taking loop bearings. By the end of the course I had still only amassed a total of 32 flying hours.

I had become friendly with a fellow cadet from Essex called Fred. He was married and a few years older that most of us, a man of experience. We had a mutual interest in boating on the River Wye and spent many hilarious times in Hereford on the river and in the numerous pubs which abounded in the city. My brother had also done his training at Madley and had briefed me on the drinking and eating places to visit in nearby Hereford. One of them was the *Racehorse*, where brother Bill had formed a close relationship with the landlord's daughter. So I introduced myself and she seemed delighted to meet me and in no time at all I had my feet under the table in a manner of speaking, following in my brother's footsteps. I persuaded the landlord's daughter to find a friend for Fred, and the girls were happy to spend their time off with us, showing us the beauties of the Herefordshire countryside amongst other things. Many a happy evening was spent at the *Racehorse*, followed by a meal at our favourite eating place, the *Devil's Kitchen*, a popular cafe on the outskirts of the city, before returning by bus to the dismal confines of the camp.

'Line-shoot' in front of visiting jets

At last the great day arrived when all the theoretical exams and practical flying tests had been successfully passed and we were presented with our Sergeant's stripes and brevets. This was one advantage of being aircrew. We didn't have to go through the usual promotional ladder of Leading Aircraftman and Corporal, but a straight jump from cadet to Sergeant. More celebrations and fond farewells to the girls, before we were on our way to No. 5 Air Navigation School at Jurby in the Isle of Man. It was here that we were to fly as fully fledged radio operators with cadet navigators.

10. JURBY

No. 5 Air Navigation School

Here we acted as Staff Wireless Operators on the faithful old Ansons, with the trainee pupils as Navigators. Fred had been posted elsewhere and I struck up a friendship with Dickie Bird, a Brummie with a broad accent from the Potteries area. He also was married but was not averse to the odd date with one of the local girls. I meanwhile had met a ravishing redhead called Moira at one of the local dance halls, and it wasn't long before I was asked round to meet her parents and have a meal. They no doubt wanted to see what sort of fellow was taking their daughter out. I must have passed the test for we continued to see a lot of each other and I became very fond of her.

My flying hours were now mounting up as I was doing three and four hour trips each day and life was good. When I was not seeing Moira, I was out boating with Dickie around the coastline by the headland, or taking a trip up the mountain to see the TT Races, and spend the day watching the riders at high speeds approaching the bridge at the end of the Sulby Straight. One or two did not brake in time and went over the wall, fortunately without serious injury.

Occasionally, I would be fortunate enough to wangle a flight to Lincolnshire, when the O/C Flying took an Anson for a weekend to Binbrook, not far from his home. This was ideal for me and I worked my passage as WOP and was able to go home and visit my parents. By now the war was over and I had mixed feelings about my service career. I was flying at last and enjoying it, and considered signing on with two of my friends. But common sense prevailed and at that stage was determined to return to the Bank when I was demobbed. I had already been in the RAF nearly three years and felt it was time for resettlement in civvy street. Yet another move and a fond farewell to Moira with a hope that one day we would meet again.

Ramsey Harbour

11. TOPCLIFFE

No. 1 Air Navigation School

It was during this time that my Sergeant's stripes were exchanged for the badges of Signaller Two, but I did retain my Signaller's brevet. My duties were to act as Staff Radio Operator on the Ansons and Wellingtons, in which the navigation cadets did their training. Topcliffe was one of the old original permanent stations with excellent facilities and the previous occupants were a bunch of high-spirited Canadians who were returning to their homeland. They had certainly left their marks in the nature of rock-hard chewing gum stuck under tables, chairs and anywhere they could get rid of it.

I was billeted in the Sergeants' Mess, sharing a room with one of my buddies, Bish, who was as mad as a hatter. Normally a quiet sort, he could become a Jekyll and Hyde character, particularly when he had a few drinks. He had an annoying habit of returning from a night out and tipping people out of their beds and generally creating havoc, but the following morning was his usual laid-back unassuming self, denying all knowledge of the previous evening's activities. I well remember one occasion when we were on our way to bed and Bish, seeing a fire bucket on the landing, emptied the contents over two pilots talking below. Fortunately for him he wasn't caught as he fled the scene at great speed. Together with Jock, an ex-British Rail employee, we made an inseparable trio and invariably went out together on the town. Jock was from Edinburgh and had a great sense of humour, but was likely to become excitable and aggressive after a drink or two.

WOP's position in Anson

Strangely enough, although Jock had a girlfriend back home it was Bish, who had no romantic ties, who was the first to become involved with a WAAF. In fact he insisted in bringing her back to the Sergeants' Mess late at night to spend the night with him, whilst I just turned the other way and let them get on with it. Eventually, these illegal happenings were reported by some unknown character, probably envious that he was not in the same position. The visits stopped and Bish was brought back into the fold of single, devil-may-care types, with two prime interests, flying and drinking. Girls were a lowly third, but it wasn't long before they moved up in the pecking order.

For a short time, I was attached to the Motor Transport section during staff shortages and I became responsible for driving the station ambulance and spent boring, monotonous hours on stand-by duty. These were relieved from time to time by emergency exercises, when the alarm sounded and I had three minutes flat to start the old Albion ambulance and drive hell-for-leather to the Control Tower. Fortunately there were no real incidents during my spell of duty, apart from a hairy ride to a Mental Hospital near York to take a crazy airman who had gone berserk with a chopper in the Officers' Mess. It took two hefty fellows to hold him down, give him an injection, and escort him in the back of the ambulance. After that episode, I was glad to get back on flying duties. Most of the pilots were battle-scarred veterans, including several Poles, who had been on operations during the war and were waiting for their demobilisation.

Ted Poludniak and some of the lads

One of them, Ted Poludniak, had an excellent baritone voice and would lead the singing in the Mess as well as teaching us Polish marching songs and romantic ballads. Another was 'Zak' Zawodny, a daring pilot with typical handlebar moustache. One of his favourite tricks on returning from a navigation trip in an Anson, was to circle over a nearby Polish Resettlement Camp, where he had many friends, and deliberately put the Anson into a steep climb until it stalled and dived straight for the camp. He then levelled out and landed, but his exploits were frowned upon by the C.O. and senior officers. But did he care? No, he would be going home soon to his beloved homeland or staying in England, where he had met an English girl. I didn't know about these goings on and when I was due to fly with Zak, he didn't enlighten me. It wasn't until we returned to base and I was relaxing that the old Anson shot upwards then started shaking like a leaf, before the stall set in and down we went in a steep dive before landing normally. Zak just grinned and asked me if I had enjoyed my trip.

In the course of one of the night navigational exercises, six Wellingtons took off around midnight on a six hour trip, which included a turning point over the North Sea and Northern France. Only five aircraft returned and to this day no one knows what happened. No distress signals were heard and no wreckage was ever found. There were far-fetched rumours of them flying over to Russia, but a more likely solution was that one of the crew members who liked to have a cigarette whilst flying, lit up and ignited fuel vapour, causing the aircraft to explode. This incident was a talking point for some time and even the local press eagerly printed a story of the aircraft which disappeared.

Another disaster occurred when a Wellington took off and for some unaccountable reason went into a steep climb, stalled, and dived down to earth, crashing and exploding in a nearby field. One lucky survivor managed to bail out and the rest, including a member of the ground staff, were killed. This was a sobering moment for me, as we dashed to the wreckage, but there was nothing that could be done. After a day in hospital, the surviving member was immediately put back on flying duties, as is the normal practice, to ensure that he didn't lose his nerve. Following this incident, which was reported in the national press, I had a telephone call, from Paddy, checking to see if I had been involved in the crash. Not long after this, one of the Wellingtons had to 'ditch' in the North Sea, suffering from engine trouble, but fortunately all of the crew members survived and were rescued, following their distress call.

Wellington landed wheels up

Just before Christmas, one of the aircraft was detailed to fly over to Belfast, ostensibly on a navigational exercise, but in reality to collect a batch of turkeys for the Officers' Mess. Landing at Aldergrove, the Wellington took on board the Christmas fare and documents changed hands. The navigator and I were responsible for loading the booty and decided to stash two turkeys in the rear turret. On returning to Topcliffe, the birds were duly unloaded and taken to their destination. Later in the evening, we visited the hangar in darkness, retrieved our turkeys, wrapped them up and posted them the next day to our respective homes. They apparently arrived in good condition and were consumed with no questions asked. However, questions were asked at the Officers' Mess, when a recount showed the documented total minus two. Although fingers of suspicion were pointed in the direction of the Sergeants' Mess, investigations revealed nothing and we breathed a sigh of relief.

Like any other RAF Station, Topcliffe had its share of bad luck when another disaster occurred, two Wellingtons returning from a navigation exercise at night collided over the airfield, with the flaming wreckage falling on the Sergeants' Mess. Fortunately there were no casualties on the ground but there were no survivors from either of the aircraft. Yet another incident involved a Wellington, which had undercarriage problems and had to land 'wheels up'. Part of the port propeller broke off on landing and went through the cockpit, embedding itself in the pilot's thigh. Luckily he survived, though the aircraft was badly damaged. In spite of these mishaps, flying continued apace and I found myself airborne most days, volunteering if I was not detailed to fly. There was always someone willing to stand down and spend the time in the snooker room, a popular place with most of the aircrew types.

With Jock and Bish, I spent my leisure hours in the evening sampling the pubs in the area at Ripon, Harrogate, Thirsk, and the occasional weekend in York. On one such occasion, a coach was hired for a day trip to Scarborough, where we had a few problems.

After a day on the beach, we retired to a pub before boarding the coach, but were delayed by the disappearance of two of the party. One of them was the proud owner of an MG sports car, which was in need of new wheels, so, spotting an identical model, decided to steal two. They were seen rolling the wheels along the street towards the coach, but before they could reach safety, they were overtaken by the local police and promptly taken to the police station with the evidence. No doubt the case against them would have been

GEOFF LENTHALL

'drunk in charge of a wheel.' The rest of the party in the
coach followed them and after a couple of hours, one of our
spokesmen managed to 'sweet-talk' the police into believing it
was just a high-spirited prank. It was gone two in the
morning when we returned to base after an exhausting and
interesting day.

On one of his previous trips into York, Jock had met a
WAAF from one of the nearby RAF stations and was in
contact with her most weekends. Bish and I used to pull his leg
about her and in the course of conversation Jock suggested
that the three of us went to York, and he would arrange for
two of his girlfriend's colleagues to join them and make up a
'blind date.' It was alright for Jock, he knew what he was
getting, but we were not so sure who we would end up with.
Jock said, "Don't worry about it, it's just the same for them.
After all, neither of you are oil paintings." We ignored his
remark and set about making arrangements for the coming
weekend. With shoes and buttons highly polished and fancying
our chances, we caught the bus to Thirsk station and boarded
the train for York. Conversation centred round the anticipated
meeting and what we planned to do, though there was some
disagreement as to whether we should join forces or go our
own way. On arrival in York, we made our way to the NAAFI
Club, where we had arranged to meet. Sure enough, on target,
were the three girls looking very smart and attractive in their
uniforms. By an amazing coincidence, I couldn't believe my
luck when I saw Paddy, the attractive red-head I had originally
met in Manchester. I said straight away, "The red-head's
mine," and Bish didn't demur, as he was left with a good-
looking blonde. Whether the girls had made any decision on
seeing them, was not known as the matter was quickly settled.
Introductions were made and after preliminary discussions
over drinks, Jock said with a twinkle in his eye, that he had
already made his plans and Bish opted for a look around York
Minster and the shops. Paddy and I decided to go for a row on
the river past Bishopthorpe.

Although we had been in touch, I hadn't realised that she had recently been posted to Lindholme. We just picked up the threads as if it were only a week since we had last seen each other. I rowed for about a quarter of an hour, then pulled into the riverbank in a secluded spot and we went ashore. As we lay side by side in the warm sunshine, I realised that I was beginning to fall in love with Paddy. She was an attractive girl with a lovely figure, a sense of humour, and we had a lot of things in common. I kissed her tenderly, this time without first asking her and my kiss was returned with affection and passion and I had the feeling that she felt the same way about me. I knew that back in London, she was going out with someone she had known for a long time and was a friend of the family.

At that time she said that he was no more than a friend and that their only real bond was the Catholic Church, which she attended regularly. Although I went to the Church of England on Church Parades, I had no strong religious convictions and if necessary I could no doubt convert to Catholicism. These were serious thoughts passing through my mind and I pulled myself together, thinking that the future lay a long way ahead and for the present I was on a blind date, though not so blind in my case. We eventually climbed back into the boat and I rowed back to the boathouse. We had arranged to meet the others back at the NAAFI Club and found the four of them waiting, eager to hear where they had been and what they had been doing.

Bish and his date had discovered that they had a mutual interest in antiques and had been wandering round the many antique shops, making one or two purchases, whilst Jock and his friend had been content to visit the Minster, see a few shops, and have a meal and a few drinks. We all stayed at the NAAFI Club where we had arranged a rendezvous, until it was time to return to base. Fond farewells were said at the station, with promises to meet again as soon as possible, and the trio boarded the train back to Thirsk station, before hitching a lift back to Topcliffe. In the Sergeants' Mess we had a few beers and discussed our day's activities. Whilst Jock and Bish were happy to talk about their day, I was a little reluctant to discuss my feelings for Paddy as I knew I would be subjected to the usual banter when anyone showed signs of becoming seriously involved with a girl. And there was no doubt about it, I was becoming seriously involved and my feelings were confused. Why couldn't I be like my mates and just go out with girls for the fun of it and whatever they had to offer? And I had already heard what Bish's girlfriend had to offer, from what Paddy had told me. Trust Bish, the dark horse. You never know about these quiet ones. Our discussion went on until the early hours in my room, where more beer was consumed, and it was nearly three in the morning when we staggered off to bed.

Fountains Abbey

Fortunately the next day was Sunday, when we had a lie in, getting up in time for a game of snooker, then lunch. A friend of ours, Ted Poludniak, a Polish pilot, had offered to take us to Fountains Abbey for the afternoon and an hour or two rowing on the river. Ted did most of the rowing, not being in the semi-comatose condition of the others, whilst we just sat back enjoying the sunshine and calling to the girls on the river bank. Bish took it into his head to volunteer to row, and in trying to change positions with Ted, managed to fall overboard. Panic stations ensued as we all tried to pull him on board, much to the amusement of onlookers enjoying a quiet walk along the tow-path. He was hauled on board, dripping wet, complaining that he had lost his pipe. He stripped off, wringing out his clothes as best he could and they returned to the mooring stage, where they had a few funny looks at the half-naked man holding a soggy bundle of clothing.

Dick and I on the river

The winter of 1947 was one of the worst for many years and in January heavy falls of snow made the runways impassable. Orders were given for everyone who was sound in body and limb to take a shovel and attempt to clear the runways. It seemed great fun at the time and everyone was enthusiastic, but after a couple of days it was realised that the snow was settling again thicker than ever and it was a losing battle against Mother Nature. The operation was abandoned and the station more or less closed down and all the aircrew were sent home on indefinite leave.

12. HOME LEAVE

Heavy snow – flying cancelled

This was welcomed, particularly by me and my friends, and I eventually made my way home by train to my home town, whilst Jock and Bish made their way to Edinburgh and Bournemouth respectively. My parents thanked me for the turkey, which had apparently arrived safe and sound by post. They were curious as to how I had acquired it but they were told it had fallen off the back of an aircraft. I spent nearly three weeks wallowing in home comforts once again and visiting the local pubs and dance halls, where I met several of my old friends who were also on leave. I well remembered going to the Berkeley Hotel with Pete, an old friend from my ATC days, who was a pilot in the Fleet Air Arm, and getting involved with a group of crazy Polish fighter pilots who had been drinking all the evening. They were tossing coins all over the dance floor then diving to retrieve as many as possible. They were charming individuals with a nice line in patter to chat up the local girls, who were only too willing to seek the company of these dashing war-scarred veterans.

Pete and I hardly got a look in but were happy enough to have a few drinks and learn one or two Polish marching songs. Pete had his eye on a girl called Mary, who was apparently a regular visitor. She was an attractive brunette with a stunning figure and Pete, fuelled by several beers and a generous dose of Dutch courage, approached the group she was standing with. Three of them were Poles, also the worse for drink, and Pete made an attempt to take his dream girl on to the dance floor, only to be set upon by the inebriated Polish aircrew. In the end I had to drag him away before any blood flowed and we retired to another of the hotel bars for one for the road before wending our weary way home, some two miles away. It had been a good night and Pete's only regret was that he wasn't walking home with Mary instead of me. He would have her next time, he told me.

On their next visit to one of the local dance halls, it was I who spotted this fair-haired girl with the most beautiful blue eyes and sylph-like figure. We both watched her from the bar and after a couple of beers I plucked up courage to ask her for a dance. She was a dream to dance with and although I was not a particularly good dancer, felt that I was on a par with Victor Sylvester. Meanwhile, Peter, who had been keeping an eye on us and looked on in amazement at some of the intricate steps we were performing, had started talking to two girls who had come to buy drinks. Not one to miss a chance, he was on the first stage of his chat-up routine, when the dance finished and I returned to finish my drink. Introductions were made all round and it was obvious that Peter had taken a fancy to Jackie, who likewise was very much taken by his good looks and easy charm. Jackie's friend Tina was approached by a friend of hers and left them for a dance.

Not wishing to be the odd one out, I was searching the room for 'Miss Blue Eyes', who was sitting with a friend on the other side of the room. I downed my drink and made my way over to her and asked her for a dance. She smiled at me, gratefully accepted my invitation, and melted into my arms as we entered into a slow foxtrot. Not being such a fast worker as my friend Peter, I was quite content just to enjoy her company and feel her warm body next to mine. It wasn't until the end of the dance that I asked her if she would like a drink. By this time Peter had his arm round Jackie and was oblivious to what was happening around him. Tina had disappeared with her ex-boyfriend and I found a cosy corner to sit down with my partner with our drinks. I introduced myself and found out that her name was Audrey. She worked in an estate agent's office and lived in the same area as I did. We found conversation easy and were beginning to feel as if we had known each other for many years (where had I heard that before?). At the end of the evening, we met up with Peter and Jackie, and Peter offered to take Jackie home and give Audrey and I a lift to her home, where I got out and escorted her to the door. I put my arms around her, gave her a gentle kiss and promised to see her again.

Bill and I on leave

The severe winter weather continued and I was delighted that I had not received my recall to resume flying duties. I was enjoying my extended leave too much. Later the next day an old friend called round unexpectedly. His name was Neil and he had been over in Canada for training as a pilot and was having a few days' leave before going to Operational Training Unit. He was the proud owner of an ancient Austin Seven and suggested we had a trip over to Burton on Stather to see a friend and have a few drinks. Their mutual friend Johnny was home on leave after serving in the Army overseas and conversation was more in the nature of a 'line-shooting' competition.

As time passed and the liquor flowed, Johnny, who knew the area very well, suggested to Neil that he ought to take a short cut on his way home. It was more of a 'dare' than a suggestion and Neil, not being one to decline a challenge, had another drink and stood up, saying, "OK lads, who is joining me on this rally across the Gobi Desert?" Well, it wasn't quite the Gobi Desert, but a stretch of land known by the locals as 'Akkies Warren', covered in bushes, trees and grass, with muddy tracks, which if you were lucky, would take you right across to the other side, coming out near the northern boundaries of the town of Scunthorpe. Waving farewell to Johnny, Neil and I set off singing lustily and started out pretty well until, taking a sloping bend too quickly, the old faithful Austin gave in and fell over on its side, throwing its occupants in a heap. We climbed out, unhurt but giggling like little schoolboys, and set about putting the old jaloppy back on its four wheels. This achieved, we got in and pressed on, none the worse for our experience, reaching home in the early hours.

13. BACK TO TOPCLIFFE

Airborne once more

I had been home for three weeks and was not surprised when, next day, my recall came through the post. It had been a good leave and I had seen quite a few of my old friends. On the way back to Topcliffe, on the crowded train from Doncaster to York, I got into conversation with a girl in the ATS, who lived in Scunthorpe and was returning to her unit in York.

Passengers were packed like sardines in the corridors and feeling tired and exhausted, I was not in a particularly sociable mood, but she was a pretty girl and seemed to want to talk to someone. It turned out that she had known my brother before he joined up and before long we were conversing like old friends. Before leaving the train at York, we exchanged names and addresses and arranged to meet in York the following weekend. During the rest of the journey to Topcliffe, I was in a contemplative mood and began to have doubts about my future. I enjoyed meeting other girls and found their company stimulating, and got round to thinking that probably my friends were right when they told me not to get tied down with anyone serious and to enjoy life – 'eat, drink and be merry, for tomorrow you may die.' I had to admit that they had the answer to life, for the time being anyway.

It was good to see Bish again, he had been living it up in Bournemouth until he got bored and decided to spend a few days in London, where he met up with the WAAF he had become friendly with in York. There were no signs of Jock, who arrived the next day, having been caught up in atrocious weather conditions in Scotland. Jock had apparently been seeing quite a lot of one of his old girlfriends, who was a devout Catholic. He had even been to church with her, which was quite an occasion for him. Bish and I were worried about the situation and decided that we must have a serious talk with him. We retired to the Sergeants Mess for a few beers and tried to show him the error of his ways, but he would not be moved. He was quite serious about the girl and was prepared to change his religion, such as it was, by re-mustering as he put it, to Catholicism. In fact he had already visited the priest for his first invocation. His attitude however, didn't interfere with his social activities and he was soon back into the happy service life with the lads. His skill on the snooker table had not diminished and he still played a tricky game on the left wing for the aircrew football team. So all was not lost.

'Wimpy' coming in to land

The weather was improving, the runways were clear, and soon life was back to normal, as flying continued *ad infinitum*. This occasionally involved taking part in air displays at various RAF Stations and I volunteered to go down to Hullavington, where they required a Wellington for static display. With a Polish pilot at the controls, we had no sooner reached 10,000 feet when the starboard engine packed up and the plane began to lose height rapidly. The pilot quickly regained control and called up base to request an emergency landing. This was my second dicey experience, but I had faith in the pilot, who brought the Wellington down in a brilliantly executed single-engine landing. Fortunately the fire engine and 'blood wagon' were not required on this occasion.

Another open day was taking place at Little Rissington in Gloucestershire, and they had put in a request for a Wellington to be flown down and put on display. *Sounds like a good day out*, I thought, and volunteered to fly as WOP for the trip. The pilot, with whom I was quite friendly, asked me to sit with him in the cockpit in the co-pilot's position. He said he knew the way and didn't need a navigator or wireless operator. I willingly agreed and after take-off he suggested that I take over for a while in the dual control position. I was no pilot and had only once been at the controls of an Anson but he didn't seem concerned and told me to keep an eye on the compass and just fly a steady course towards our destination. Before landing he took over and we spent an interesting day at the show before setting off back to Topcliffe. He told me what to do prior to take off and said to me, "Right, it's all yours, take her away." Little did he know that he was taking his life in my hands, but he seemed to have faith so off we went. Throttles forward, gathering speed, ease the stick forward to raise the tail then at take-off speed he said, "OK, stick back gently and off we go." Sounds easy, but my use of the rudder was somewhat erratic and before take-off we were swerving from side to side until I got the hang of it. Having taken off with the odd bit of adjustment from the pilot, we climbed to 8,000 feet and headed for base. He seemed quite happy to let me fly back but of course when we approached Topcliffe, he took over. He wasn't prepared to let me land the plane and I don't blame him. The consequences could have been disastrous.

A week before Jock, Bish and I were due to be demobbed, yet another demob party took place in Ripon in the time-honoured manner of a pub crawl. Apart from an aggressive incident when Jock had to be pulled away from two Army types who had a disagreement with him, it was a hilarious evening, with much laughter and some bawdy singing. At closing time, the trio, much the worse for wear, made their uncertain way to the railway station, where they hoped to catch the last train to Topcliffe. On the way Bish decided to chat up two WAAFs and was seen pointing to the sky, apparently giving them a lecture on navigating by the stars and naming the various constellations. When he was heard to say '*Castor and Pollux*', we dragged him away and he promptly made for the river and started climbing up one of the bridge supports. After a struggle, we escorted him, one on each side, to the station. The train was in and due to depart any minute and we scrambled into the carriage with only minutes to spare. Bish decided to try and go to sleep on the luggage rack and with difficulty we managed to get him down and also prevent him from pulling the communication cord to stop the train. In due course, the train drew to a halt at the last station before Thirsk and Bish said he was getting out. Before anyone could stop him, he had opened the door on the track side and jumped down. I called out and promptly followed him to get him on board again, but Bish had other plans. He was determined to disconnect the carriage and tried to lift the anchoring connection between the carriages, but as he struggled the whistle blew and I had to pull him out as the train drew slowly away from the station.

Our efforts to climb aboard the moving train were unsuccessful and we stood on the track watching Jock hanging out of the window waving them goodbye. We decided that there was only one thing for it and that was to walk along the track, some five miles or so to our destination at Thirsk. Hearing irate cries from the Stationmaster, we set off at a run until we were out of earshot. After an hour or so, we arrived at the station and made our way to Topcliffe, looking bedraggled and feeling weary from our exertions. In the Sergeants' Mess a party was still in progress and Bish and I entered to wild cheers from our friends, who said they had contemplated sending out a search party. After telling them our story, we had a well-earned drink or two, then staggered off to bed, to sleep soundly.

14. ON A FIZZER!

In trouble, demob party, Lakenheath – final flight

We knew that the day would soon dawn when we should be leaving this way of life to return to our mundane occupations and arranged a pre-demob session in Ripon. This was by way of a taster for the finale and when we returned to camp Bish suggested that it might be a good idea to say goodnight to the Station Warrant Officer. He went to the telephone and I stood by listening, not realising at first that his intention was to ring the fire brigade to tell them that the SWO's house was on fire. Shortly afterwards we heard the siren and bells of the fire engine and hurriedly made our way to bed. The following morning we heard that two pilots had been arrested and blamed for the hoax message, as they were seen near the telephone fooling around. After a discussion we decided to confess our sins (me for aiding and abetting) and reported to the guardroom and put on a charge. Quick march, left, right, left, right, caps off, etc., you know the drill. We were both severely reprimanded and placed in custody and spent the weekend in the 'glasshouse.' Our colleagues thought it hilarious when they saw us being marched to and from meals escorted by SPs but we weren't so happy. We did not sleep at all well on the hard floor. Freedom came on Monday when we were released and we rejoined our buddies for a welcoming drink. An appropriate greetings card was presented to us depicting a fire engine attending a house fire and signed by all the lads. That blotted our copybook.

Eventually the penultimate day of our service in the RAF arrived and we decided to spend the evening in Harrogate with several of our friends for our final demob party. The occasion was both happy and sad and after a tour of the watering holes, we made our way back to the station to catch the train, and during the course of conversation Bish said that he would like to have one final flight before we left for the demob centre the following morning. Jock and I, in a mellow frame of mind, readily agreed, and on our return to Topcliffe, we went to the crew room to try and wangle our final flight. Much to our surprise, there was no opposition and three wireless operators who were detailed for flying were only too happy to stand down. We collected our flying gear, attended briefing, and shortly after midnight the Wellingtons were airborne and heading for the first turning point of the six-hour navigational exercise. Poor old Bish was feeling under the weather, but after he was sick, he managed to carry on with his duties. Unfortunately, on returning to base, thick fog had settled in over most of Yorkshire and we were unable to land, being diverted to Linton-on-Ouse. Heading for Linton at a reduced height on Standard Beam Approach, the Wellington in which I was flying was approaching Sutton Bank, when I heard over the intercom the words, "Christ Almighty," uttered by the Polish pilot in an alarmed manner.

Suddenly the aircraft climbed at a very steep angle with the engines at full throttle and the pilot's voice was heard again. "Bloody hell, that was a near thing." Apparently he had just made out the outline of Sutton Bank in the fog and took violent evasive action. Throttling back, we made for Linton-on-Ouse, only to be told that the fog had thickened and were again diverted to Lakenheath in Suffolk. By this time fuel was getting low and we eventually landed there, having been airborne for over seven hours.

Shortly after landing, two other aircraft landed, having also been diverted, and Jock, Bish and I were reunited in the Sergeants' Mess. After debriefing, we had a hearty breakfast and slept soundly until mid-day. When we looked out of the window we couldn't believe that the fog had descended over Suffolk and a return to Topcliffe was impossible. We had been billeted in the Station Sick Quarters and were well looked after, like VIPs. That night at the bar, we discussed the situation and realised that our diversion would put paid to our demob the following day. Little did we know that it would be a week before the fog lifted sufficiently for us to return to base. In the meantime, we collected some pay from nearby Mildenhall and had a relaxing time as guests at Lakenheath until the weather conditions improved.

This unexpected diversion and the continued bad weather gave us plenty of time to think about the future, particularly the immediate future, when we eventually had to return to Topcliffe. In the first place we should never have been flying at all on the night before our demob, particularly in the inebriated state that we must have been. Secondly, we had upset the system in the administration department and they would not be too happy about the situation. Would we face another charge? Anyway, there was no point in worrying about it, we should soon find out on our return to face the music.

15. RETURN TO TOPCLIFFE

Final demob and high jinks in London

On our return to Topcliffe, we were welcomed back by our colleagues who thought they had seen the last of us. Naturally, questions were asked as to why we were flying on the last night before our demob and the Admin Officer was not too pleased with the situation as all the paperwork for our demob had to be sorted out for a future date. We were not too popular in certain administration quarters. Whether or not it was a deliberate plot, we did not find out, but the facts were that we had to spend nearly another three months there, during which time we flew nearly every day. Possibly the service method of punishing those who upset the system, but we didn't mind as we enjoyed flying and the social life, and were not particularly looking forward to returning to civvy street. During this extended spell we all managed to wangle seven days' leave and spent many more happy evenings in Ripon, Harrogate, Thirsk, and York. A week before the revised demob date we were given strict instructions not to fly on our final night and instead we had a second demob party in Ripon, finishing off in the Sergeants' Mess.

The big day arrived and we made our way to the Demob Centre just outside Blackpool, handing in all our Service gear (well, most of it) and left, feeling slightly embarrassed in the regulation grey pinstripe suits, trilby hats and raincoats. Instead of returning to our respective homes, we decided to spend a week in London in a final fling before returning to our jobs. We made our base at the Brevet Club in Piccadilly, making sorties to various places of entertainment, including Soho and trips to the theatres. After a lunch-time drinking session, we were in mellow mood and decided that we didn't really want to return to our boring jobs and visited the American Embassy, where we had interviews and collected forms with a view to joining the USAAF to fight in Korea. In addition we gathered information on working as Ground Radio Operators in Germany. On our final night in the capital, in a none too sober state, we pledged lifetime friendship and drank a toast to the future, whatever it may hold. When we arrived home in the cold light of day, I rejoined the bank, Bish went back to the estate agency, and Jock returned to his job on the railways. So much for joining the USAAF and doing our bit for the Americans.

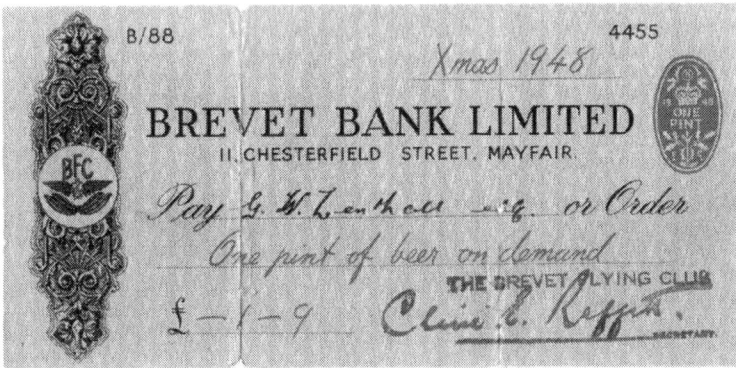

A cheap pint at the Brevet Club

It was an unsettling time for all returning members of the Armed Forces, trying to integrate into civilian life after years of Service life, exciting times and great fellowship. Bish particularly had his problems. The girl he had left behind had married and left the area, and life in the Estate Agency was humdrum in the extreme. The staff had changed and he didn't have a lot in common with them, added to which his own feelings and enthusiasm for the job were not what they were. After several boring and frustrating months, he left and started a new job as a ground radio operator at one of the civil airports. He was much happier there, but sadly his mind began to be affected by the constant operation of the Morse code and he finished up in a mental hospital, where sadly, he died within two years of leaving the RAF.

Meanwhile, Jock had returned to his administration job on the railways and gradually settled into his old routine. He was joyfully reunited with his girlfriend and completed his conversion course for the Catholic faith. They married within six months, but not before he had returned to Topcliffe for the occasional reunion weekends where we met up with old friends and celebrated in our accustomed style. With a few words in the right quarters, we wangled accommodation in the Sergeants' Mess and ate with our old friends in the Mess. Jock eventually became the father of two boys, who grew up to be excellent footballers like their father.

16. HOME AGAIN

Return to the bank

I reluctantly returned to the bank, picking up the threads of my former career. I was living at home with my parents and was just beginning to settle down when, after just over a year, I was transferred from Scunthorpe to the Grimsby branch of the bank, where I moved into digs with two other bankers. One was with Barclays and the other at the same branch as I was. They were both ambitious and the three of us spent most evenings studying for the Bankers' Institute examinations.

Ken, from Barclays, was eventually transferred to one of their overseas branches and ultimately finished up as General Manager of Unicorn Trust, one of Barclays' subsidiaries. We understood that, prior to his promotion, he struck up a friendship, which eventually resulted in marriage, to the daughter of one of the bank directors. Maurice, at Westminster, was transferred to Leicester branch where he was married on the same day as Joan and I. He too was obviously in the top echelon and ended his days as General Manager (Domestic Banking) of the Westminster bank.

So where did I go wrong? My close association with such ambitious types should have rubbed off on me, but alas, no, I wasn't in the same league. In our spare time we visited the local pub in Ken's battered old Riley car, which had seen better days, but nevertheless transported us in our hour of need for the odd glass of beer or two.

Life was good for me and my banking colleagues, living in digs with 'the merry widow' as we called our landlady. It was a free and easy existence and I still received the occasional telephone call from Paddy, the Irish girl I had become friendly with in York. She was still in the WAAFs stationed at Cranwell, where I arranged to go and see her. I managed to wangle accommodation in the Sergeants' Mess and we spent many happy hours reminiscing in the NAAFI Club at Sleaford, where we spent most of our time together before returning to camp. We seemed to have a rapport with each other and had a lot in common, and on my way back home to my digs, my thoughts turned to the future; although marriage had not been mentioned, I had a feeling that in due course the subject was bound to come up. Then again, I was only 23 and I had my whole life in front of me, and didn't even know whether or not I would be staying in the bank. Although it was a steady, secure job with good prospects, I had a gut feeling that it was not really the career for me. Invariably, after these weekends away, there were the typical bawdy and suggestive comments from my colleagues about my activities and my firm replies that it was a purely platonic friendship were greeted with hoots of derision.

Progress in the bank was painfully slow, and though I enjoyed my work as a cashier, my efforts in studying for the Banking Examinations were not bearing a lot of fruit. In fact, although I passed three exams one year and only one the next, my endeavours appeared to be getting me nowhere. Bank inspections were never looked forward to as the final interviews and assessments always led to the same question about my unsuccessful efforts at the Bankers' Institute examinations. I had a feeling that I never made a very good impression and all these details would go on a report to Head Office.

The Manager at Riby Square was popular and a bit of a character. He used to go down to London for the occasional weekend with one of his customers. He would return looking as if he had enjoyed a hectic weekend and I well remember seeing his cheques issued in London come through with a shaky signature, obviously having been written whilst under the influence. He was addicted to filling in football coupons and every Friday he could be seen entering his crosses on the coupon. One of us was then asked to go to the post office for a postal order to send off his winning entry. He told me once that he had been sending entries in for 20 years and never had a win. One of his words of wisdom to me was never to have a joint account with your wife. He said that I would earn the money and my wife would spend it. He followed his own advice to me by having separate accounts for himself and his wife.

The bank had a sub-branch on the docks and I had to take a taxi with the cash and a security guard for protection. He was usually retired and I sometimes wondered how he would cope if any emergency arose. Fortunately in those days, bank raids were not so prevalent and he just sat on a chair having a smoke and chatting to the customers. Every Tuesday was 'settlement day' when all the fish merchants settled up their debts to each other by a form of voucher. The merchants came into the bank in all their fish dock gear, smelling to high heaven, and paid in their filthy notes, covered in fish scales and reeking of fish. Being in charge of a sub-branch wasn't such a bad deal as you could do your own thing if it was not too busy – no manager or chief clerk looking over your shoulder. I remember one such branch where the previous cashier stored his 'girlie' magazines in one of the drawers, which made for interesting reading and helped to pass the time.

17. RAF VOLUNTEER RESERVE

Signing on for five years

I had joined the Volunteer Reserve for a five year contract
after my demob as my love of flying was still very strong and I
had to admit to myself that I was missing it, together with the
comradeship of the Services. Most weekends would be spent at
Doncaster, flying in Ansons on navigational exercises or the
occasional flip in a Tiger Moth, with a pilot who lived at
Grimsby. On these occasions I was treated to an aerial tour of
the coastal area of Cleethorpes and Grimsby with an added
bonus of an aerobatic session, including looping the loop over
the River Trent area on the way back. This was my first time
and I enjoyed it immensely. Not only was I enjoying life in the
RAFVR, but I was getting paid for it. In addition, each year I
was allowed two weeks' training at a Royal Air Force station
over and above my holiday allowance in the Bank. This was
not popular with the hierarchy in the bank, but I was not the
only one involved, as the Chief Clerk, an ex-Army major, also
took two extra weeks for training with the Territorials.

Avro Lincoln at Binbrook

Most of my training was done at Doncaster Reserve Centre but one of these occasions was spent at nearby RAF Binbrook, where I flew as a crew member of an Avro Lincoln taking part in 'Operation Bullseye', a practice bombing operation over Heligoland. On this occasion we were unable to find our target due to bad weather and our bombs were jettisoned in the North Sea. I had several trips as Radio Operator in the Avro Lincoln, including one of the longest flights I had made on a navigational exercise to Paris, down to La Rochelle and back to base. We were airborne for six and a half hours. I also had the pleasure of meeting the renowned Group Captain Hamish Mahaddie, who was later to become well known for his contributions in an advisory capacity to television companies. I enjoyed every minute of my two weeks' training and it was with a feeling of regret that I returned to my mundane job in the bank after each year's training session. Another of the highlights was a trip to Jersey at the time of the 'Battle of the Flowers'. The crew of three stayed in St. Helier at one of the best hotels, where we wined and dined in style, before visiting a night club for an evening's entertainment. The resulting hangover was quickly dealt with the following morning by a stiff dose of tomato juice with lashings of salt and pepper and Worcester sauce, well and truly mixed. Far better than banking, were my thoughts, particularly as we were getting paid for the experience.

Ansons at Doncaster

The next trip from Doncaster was a navigational flight to Buckeburg in Germany in an Anson, taking off from Doncaster and calling in at Waddington for Customs clearance, then across the North Sea to Buckeburg. It was at this time that, during the Cold War, the trigger-happy Russians shot down a British aircraft which they claimed had violated their territory near Berlin. This caused consternation back home in England to the families of those in the Anson, as they assumed that it had been shot down, but fortunately we were not involved. These trips were in the nature of navigational exercises and proved an excellent way of keeping our hand in and learning any updates in procedures. A couple of days sightseeing and evenings of hospitality in the RAF Mess passed the time quickly for the three of us, who then returned to Doncaster to finish off the remainder of our annual training, and back to the everyday grind in the world of banking.

18. LOVE ALL

The girl in red shorts at the Tennis Club

At the tennis club I was beginning to get to know some of the members and although there were some attractive girls, I found that my attentions always seemed to focus on the girl with the red shorts whom I had met before. It was some time before I, being of a shy disposition, plucked up courage to speak to her. It then became a regular routine to escort her home through People's Park, where we loitered for a while on the park bench, before we were sent on our way by the local bobby. How times have changed – these days you are more likely to be accosted by yobs or faced with a flasher in a dirty raincoat. I was attracted by her extrovert personality and zany sense of humour, and it wasn't long before I asked her out. Even though, on the face of it, we didn't appear to have a lot in common, we got on very well and the time we spent in each other's company seemed to pass very quickly.

Her name was Joan and she was a regular churchgoer at the Methodist Church, and it wasn't long before I was reluctantly accompanying her to services on Sunday mornings. Having spent most of my Sundays in the RAF on other leisure pursuits and having no strong religious convictions, I felt a little like a fish out of water, but I was invited to join the church choir. If my old buddy Jock could make a success of the transition to Catholicism, then there was no reason why I shouldn't do likewise in the Methodist Church. Apart from my experiences of somewhat bawdy singing in various pubs and the Sergeants' Mess, I was reluctant to accept, and was only persuaded by Joan and her parents, who were both in the choir. Initially I felt that I was not fully accepted, particularly when I took her out for a drive and we finished up in a pub, where she had her first shandy. Not that my life was one long alcoholic round. Far from it, for one thing I could not afford to live the life I had enjoyed in the RAF, on my meagre salary from the bank. Apart from the odd hiccup in our relationship, Joan and I got on extremely well and in due course the conversation turned to engagement. One bone of contention was the fact that I was still serving my time in the RAFVR and spending some of my weekends flying and two weeks each year at an RAF station for my annual training. Joan wanted me to give it up and said she would not think of marriage until I stopped flying. This put me on the spot as I was still enjoying the comradeship and flying during my part-time service with the RAF and I was very reluctant to give it up. In any case I had signed up for a five year period and there was no way I could resign. So life continued on those terms and eventually my service came to an end, and Joan was relieved as she had this premonition and fear that I might be involved in a flying accident.

Joan on court

19. GLIDING COURSE

A week at Tibbenham in Norfolk

Although my service with the RAFVR was over, I couldn't resist taking advantage of a course I had seen advertised for one week's gliding in Norfolk. There were six of us on the course and we stayed in a guest house close to the airfield at Tibbenham. The instructor was an ex-RAF pilot and after initial briefings we took it in turns in the dual control glider. It was a typical training machine with a Volkswagen engine, and take off was similar to a normal powered aircraft. On reaching around 2,000 feet the engine was switched off and gliding began. The instruments were basic and the search for thermals to take us higher was indicated on the altimeter.

Ready for take-off at Tibbenham

Once a thermal had been found we did our best to circle round within the area and gain height. I had taken my video camera with me and the pilot, possibly with the idea of giving me something worth taking, decided to loop-the-loop. So it's all now on film and I bore my family to tears when I offer to show them. There are loud cries of, "Oh no, not the gliding film." It was great fun, particularly on the last day when we had the opportunity to fly it ourselves, with the instructor beside us of course! One of my ambitions was to go solo in a powered plane and this is something I have put on my list of things to do when I retire properly – whenever that may be!

Later on in life I had the opportunity to have a day's gliding near Grantham. One of my friends Des, had told me that his son was a gliding instructor and we were invited to spend a day with him. On this occasion the glider was towed by a powerful Jaguar until a suitable height was reached and the hook was released. This was quite an experience and we prayed that the Jag didn't run out of petrol.

My third experience took place at Kirton Lindsey, where one of the Orpheus Choir was a club member. This time the take-off was by means of a towing winch and all I managed was about ten minutes with the instructor before an approaching storm cut short our flight. At least I had experienced three different means of take-off and all of them had been exhilarating and had the adrenalin flowing.

20. TYING THE KNOT

The great day

Joan and I were getting along fine and found that we had a lot in common and after a two year engagement, were married on September the 22nd 1951 in the local Methodist Church (I made a mental note to always remember the date for future reference, otherwise I would be in trouble). We honeymooned in Torquay, where we met six other couples from different parts of England who had married on the same day. At that time I didn't own a car and my father-in-law kindly offered his Standard Vanguard for the week. He must have had great faith in my driving abilities. We became friendly with two of the couples and kept in touch. After a blissful week we returned to our home in Compton Drive, I went back to the bank, and Joan returned to her job as Shorthand Typing teacher at the Cleethorpes College of Commerce.

The question of children eventually arose, but neither of us were particularly enthusiastic about the idea and it was four years before Joan became pregnant, more by accident than design. A little girl, Lindsay, was born and followed four years later with another girl, Carol. Naturally we were delighted, although I had said that I would like a boy who could follow in my footsteps and achieve my ambitions.

The wedding ceremony took place at George Street Methodist Church, which is alas no more. In its place is a furniture shop. The reception was held at Field House, which also has been swallowed up by a housing complex. As is the usual practice, I had to give a speech, which if I remember rightly, was short and to the point. It is on these occasions that I envied the likes of Arthur Scargill. I didn't like the fellow, but what a speaker he was. A modicum of alcohol was served although the majority of guests were Methodists. I am not proud of the fact, but I was responsible for leading Joan astray by introducing her to a shandy. Nowadays she enjoys a gin and tonic, wine and even the odd beer. How times have changed!

Our Wedding Day

Now that the attachment to flying was finally severed, I resumed my studies for the Banking examinations, though with little success. I was taking a correspondence course with the Rapid Results College but on this occasion the results were certainly not rapid. Meanwhile my colleagues had departed, having been transferred to branches elsewhere. One of my friends in the branch was a keen footballer and after many discussions over a pint or two at the Wheatsheaf, we decided to start a Banks soccer team and after circularising the other banks, were successful in finding sufficient numbers to form a team, with the additional support of one or two from outside the banking industry. With the exception of Mac, a wee wiry Scot on the left wing and Jim, a staunch stopper centre half, who were both experienced players, the remainder were a motley crew of average players. With the help of several of the managers, who were appointed Vice-Presidents and donated the handsome sum of two guineas each to club funds, we were able to purchase shirts and shorts and launched into Division Five of the local league. Progress was slow but enjoyable and firm bonds of friendship were made. Team selection took place at the Wheatsheaf Hotel over a beer or two, but we were never in a position to have our own ground and had to be content to play on the Council-owned Barretts or Bradley playing fields, where conditions and facilities were basic to say the least. The changing rooms were unlit and unheated, but at least they were dry and more often than not, some of the pitches were under water during the winter months. Nevertheless, they were free from cow dung, which was a none-too-pleasant feature of some of the privately owned grounds we had played on.

Eventually, due to transfers of players to other branches, the team sadly folded and the remaining players either joined other clubs or gave up the game for more leisurely pursuits. And this was the nearest I became to one of my ambitions of becoming a professional footballer. My father in his youth had played for Brigg Town, and one of his wishes had been for my brother and I to eventually play for a league club. Bill and I both played for our schools and apart from the occasional game in the RAF, that was as far as it went.

21. HITCHHIKE TO EUROPE

To escape the boredom of life in a bank, I had the urge to try something completely different for my next holiday. Talking to a friend of mine at the local badminton club, we discussed the situation and came up with the idea of visiting France for the grape harvest and earn a little money at the same time. With this in mind, we hired a tandem and spent a few days getting used to riding it. Not so easy as it may seem. We fell off several times, broke a few spokes, and reluctantly decided that there was no way that we would get very far in this country, let alone on the continent. We had already equipped ourselves with rucksacks and all the necessary paraphernalia required for such a trip. The tandem was returned and last minute arrangements enabled us to hitch a lift to London on one of McVeigh Transport's lorries based in Grimsby. This was an experience in itself as we travelled through the night, stopping at transport cafes for the odd snack and drink.

'Not far to go,' says Rowley.

We were dropped off at the Blackwall Tunnel and made our way via a succession of lifts to Maidstone, where we ate a hearty breakfast before making our way to Hythe, on the south coast. We were both members of the Youth Hostel Association and it had been our intention to use hostels throughout our journey, to save money. Sadly there was no hostel in Hythe and we stayed at a boarding house, which was much more comfortable, but of course more expensive. Here we had our last breakfast in England for a fortnight and made for Lydd, home of Silver City Airways. We had previously booked a flight on this ungainly-looking Bristol air ferry, which, in less than half an hour, had touched down on French soil at Le Touquet and we passed quickly through customs, minus tandem.

Silver City Airways

We were in high spirits, with a full two weeks ahead of us, not knowing from one day to the next where we would be staying. We had no set plan, just a rough idea of seeing as much of the continent as we could in the allotted time. Once again we were unlucky regarding a Youth Hostel and had to dig deeply into our supply of currency to pay for accommodation in a guest house overlooking the sea. The weather was beautiful and we decided to rest awhile before heading inland. This was a mistake. The good weather and proximity of the sea encouraged us to stay for a couple of days, which meant that when we reluctantly set off with light hearts, our financial situation was not as good as we had planned. In the boarding house we had met two Australian girls, Tas and Di, who were on a tour of Europe and coincidentally we would see them from time to time on our journey, as they were thumbing a lift in the same direction.

This was our first experience of hitchhiking on foreign soil and after walking for two miles, we began to think that perhaps it was not such a good idea after all. Our luck changed when we spotted a car parked in a lay-by with a GB plate. We got into conversation with the English couple, who were heading for the coast to return to England, in other words, they were going in the wrong direction for us. They kindly offered to share their lunch with us and we set off once again. This time, after only a few moments, we were picked up by a voluble Frenchman in an ancient Peugeot saloon. He seemed quite happy to chatter away, even though we hadn't the slightest idea what he was talking about, as our knowledge of French was only limited. This was one of a series of lifts which eventually brought us to the French capital.

From our map, we knew the location of a Youth Hostel and took the Metro to the area. By this time it was 9.30pm and to our dismay, it was fully booked. We were offered a plot of ground to erect a tent, but as we had decided against taking one, this wasn't the answer. At the reception area we met an English girl with her French boyfriend, who had the same problem. He suggested that the four of us went to the local police station where he spoke to one of the gendarmes, who kindly offered to put us up for the night in individual cells. During the night a group of what we assumed to be prostitutes were brought in and we couldn't believe it when they were soon swigging wine and playing cards. It was obvious that they were regular visitors and knew the drill. Although they made gestures towards us we ignored them – we were too tired and anyway we had headaches! We had never been in a French gaol and it wouldn't go down very well with the bank. After a fitful night with not much sleep, we were given a steaming cup of black coffee and croissants and 'released' without charge by the friendly gendarmes. What a start to the holiday.

Parlez-vous Anglais?

We breakfasted in a local café and made our way to the Place Vendome, where the Westminster Foreign Bank was located. We replenished our supply of francs and picked up some useful information of what to see and do in Paris. To see all the sights it is necessary to stay for a week or two and have a well lined purse. Though we covered a lot of ground including the Eiffel Tower in the short time we were there, it was exhausting and we knew we had to move on.

We headed for the outskirts of the city and took up a strategic position on one of the roads heading east. Our progress to Chalons, where the grape harvest was about to commence, was steady if not spectacular. The French authorities had thoughtfully planted fruit trees along our route and the endless supply of apples and pears, together with a flagon of wine, fortified us on our journey. Enquiries about the harvest informed us that we were too early and we had to revise our plans, which were very flexible anyway.

So, we were on our way again and were picked up by a French priest in Vitry and taken 30 miles or so before we saw this rakish-looking sports car approaching. The occupant, a young French doctor, stopped and asked us in English where we were going (he had spotted the union jacks on our rucksacks). We replied that we had no set destination and would be happy to go as far as he would take us. We climbed in and settled ourselves in the back seats with a crate of champagne sitting between us. He told us he was heading for the Vosges Mountains to meet his girlfriend, and judging by the contents on the back seat, it was going to be some celebration! This seemed to be our lucky day, as en route to Colmar, to the east of the Vosges mountain range, he pulled in to a roadside restaurant in Nancy for lunch. It was no transport café, far from it, and we felt a degree of uneasiness as we entered the high-class dining room as we could not be described as being the epitome of elegance in our shorts and open-necked shirts. Paul, as the doctor had asked us to call him, told us to order whatever we liked as the meal was on him (he had come into some money unexpectedly, he told us). We protested but he had obviously made his mind up and taken pity on his two scruffy-looking travelling companions and told us to get stuck in (or the French equivalent) and ordered a litre bottle of red wine. This was real living, we thought, as we tucked into our substantial meal and helped him to finish off the wine. He would not take a franc for the meal and later, having obtained his address, we sent him a small gift as a token of our appreciation.

Paul was an excellent driver and told us that in France they drive v*ite, vite* and he certainly did. With the roof down, we found it exhilarating driving along the mountain roads and darkness was approaching as we arrived at Colmar, some 300 kilometres from our pick-up point. This had been the longest journey we had made by hitchhiking so far, and we were very grateful. Paul wished us well as we bade him goodbye and made our way to the youth hostel, which to our delight was not full. We paid our accommodation fee, did our chores as required at all hostels, had a meal, and went to bed exhausted.

The following morning we had a discussion as to our next destination, as we had made better progress than we had anticipated, thanks to the doctor. A decision was made to head for Switzerland, where we spent the night at Basle, but I had to pay double rates as I was over age for a youth hostel (strange rules they have in Switzerland – I always thought that there was no age limit). Another evening of chores before settling down in the basic but clean accommodation to socialise with people from different countries and customs. We would liked to have seen more of Switzerland by travelling to Lucerne, but time was running out so our next objective had to be Germany.

We crossed the Swiss/German border in the early morning, and found a roadside café where we devoured a colossal ham and eggs breakfast. It cost us the equivalent of six shillings (a lot of money to us in those days) but it was well worth it. Refreshed and full of the joys of summer, we pressed on northwards to Freiburg, a cathedral town nestling between the Rhine valley and the Black Forest. It was here that the wine festivals were in full swing and we passed many gaily decorated vehicles on their way to Sunday services. During our trip we had travelled in a variety of vehicles including a waste disposal truck, but our arrival in Freiburg exceeded all our expectations as we were dropped off from a chauffeur-driven Opel limousine. It was even flying a pennant but we never did find out who the owner was, and were most surprised when the driver deigned to pick up a couple of casually dressed weary Brits. We only had time for a quick visit to the cathedral before heading north and were lucky to be picked up by a van (not quite what we had become accustomed to, but beggars can't be choosers) going all the way to Heidelberg. This was indeed a stroke of good fortune as the distance was just over 100 miles.

Heidelberg is a beautiful university town on the banks of the River Neckar, and we found time to relax and unwind, watching the boats go by. We were tempted to spend a few hours sitting in the sunshine but we were hungry and found a restaurant and sampled our first taste of pumpernickel (not impressed). Our search for a Youth Hostel was rewarded as we came across the largest one we had seen, with accommodation for 400 people. We were made welcome and decided to stay for two nights in the convivial atmosphere. The open courtyard, where hostellers of all nationalities were gathered, singing to the accompaniment of a piano accordion. It was reminiscent of a scene from *"The Student Prince"* and we soon made friends in the happy atmosphere, drinking beer from typical German steins until the late evening.

River Neckar

The following morning we took the opportunity of climbing the wooded slopes and headed for the Königstuhl, a type of funicular railway which took us the top, from where we had a magnificent view of the River Neckar threading its way through the town below. So far, the weather had been excellent and it wasn't until we left Heidelberg that our exit was accompanied by a refreshing shower, which soon passed. A consultation with our map persuaded us that our next stop should be Luxemburg. At the entry to the Autobahn we had not long to wait before we were picked up by a German lawyer, who took us across the Rhine, through industrial Mannheim (still showing the effects of bombing during the war), and on to Kaiserslautern. Due to its proximity to a large American air base, this town was known locally as 'Little America' and certainly there appeared to be more American cars than German. Whilst patiently waiting for our next lift, we were accosted by a German policeman and we immediately thought that we were in trouble. Luckily, we were wrong, as he spoke very good English and seemed happy to have a conversation. He asked us where we were going and he took it upon himself to stop passing vehicles to ask their destinations. We found this highly amusing and unexpected and soon we were on our way heading west.

We eventually reached Saarbrucken and took a tram to the suburb of Volklingen which would put us en route to Luxemburg. Taking some German deutschmarks from my pocket, I offered them to the conductor, who muttered something under his breath in German, but he took my money, giving me change in Saar francs. We had taken currencies for several countries but hadn't reckoned on passing through Saarland when we set off. Leaving the tram, we enquired from a stranger in our best German the quickest way to get to Luxemburg and were surprised when he replied in English. By a strange coincidence he had spent some time working in Lincolnshire and to prove it he said a few words in the local dialect. He was a friendly type and even invited us to tea, but we had to reluctantly decline as we hoped to reach our destination by nightfall.

It was around 8pm when we arrived at the Youth Hostel after a noisy, hectic ride in a gravel wagon (we weren't proud chaps). Luxemburg is a quaint old town with floodlit castles and towering viaducts which made a striking picture. Whilst there we came across an old London taxi cab, liberally painted with place names and humorous comments. On the roof was a prominent illuminated 'Canada' sign. The occupants, two intrepid young Canadian girls, were on their way to England, having completed a lengthy European tour.

An overnight thunderstorm had fortunately ended before we left and we didn't have to wait long before being taken to the French border. Here we met a little Frenchman, who, having seen our Union Jack, introduced himself in English. In the course of conversation he told us that he had worked in the city of Lincoln and knew our part of the country well. It's a small world. We were relieved when an American car pulled up and took us to the US air base at Etain. We couldn't believe our luck when our next road Samaritan was a Frenchman speaking fluent American who took us on a tour of the battlefields before dropping us in Verdun. It was quite an experience to meet so many friendly people who seemed only too pleased to offer assistance.

From Verdun we had another of our lucky breaks as we climbed aboard this lorry going to the docks at Le Havre. The driver was obviously an admirer of the opposite sex as his cab was covered with pin-ups, which no doubt kept his spirits up on a long journey. He dropped us at Beauvais, where, as it was my birthday, we found a place to celebrate before retiring at the local hostel. After performing our chores the following morning, we left on our final leg of the journey. Our luck seemed to have deserted us as progress was painfully slow – 45 kilometres in five hours. At Poix, we recorded our longest wait of two hours, before eventually reaching Abbeville, where we were immediately picked in a fast Panhard saloon, driven by a Cambridge educated Frenchman returning from Paris to his estate at Le Touqet. Obviously a man of some substance and wealth, but quite happy to stop and take us on board.

Back at our starting point two weeks later we booked in at the same hotel for our final night. The following day we spent what was left of our currency (which wasn't a great deal) and made our way to the airport for the return journey across the Channel. Our efforts to hitchhike back home were not nearly as successful as when we set off, but after a struggle we made it to London and Kings Cross Station. When we tried to purchase tickets, we realised that we had insufficient money and sadly had to sell my box of cigarettes which I had bought for a friend.

So, in the early hours of the morning, we arrived back in Grimsby, said our farewells, and made our way to our respective homes. I realised that I had not taken my door key with me and had to throw pebbles at the upstairs back window to wake my wife. She eventually opened the curtains and saw this tired, bedraggled, scruffy-looking creature grinning up at her and realised that it was her beloved husband. After a much needed breakfast and shower, I went to bed and zonked out for the rest of the morning.

In all we had travelled some 1,500 miles in four different countries, including a three day rest at Le Touquet, at a cost of the princely sum of £26. This of course was way back in 1955 and things have changed. It had been an exciting, stimulating experience and full of amusing events and happy memories of the spirit of international comradeship in the hostels and on the road.

22. LEICESTER

Transfer and finding a home

Just before Christmas 1961 I was transferred to St. Martins branch of the bank at Leicester and I found myself travelling back and forth, living in a hotel in Leicester and returning at weekends to Grimsby. In the hotel were two other bankers who had been transferred and were also looking for a house. This was during a bitterly cold winter and our efforts to view houses were not initially over successful. Eventually after about twelve weeks I had found a suitable house in Glenfield Road and Joan and the children settled in their new home on the outskirts of Leicester. It was a four-bedroom semi-detached situated on a main road leading to Groby, and proved ideal as a family home.

Having spent several weeks on 'the team' calculating interest amongst other mundane jobs allocated to those just joining the branch, I was transferred to the Managers' Department, a small section of four, directly responsible to the Senior Manager and his deputy. By strange coincidence, Maurice Denton, who had been in digs with me in Grimsby, was transferred from Inspection Staff to Leicester as Manager's Assistant. So we met again, but this time he was my superior, although he was quite friendly but conscious of his position. There were nearly one hundred members on the staff and it was here that I met Peter, a real 'character' with a great sense of humour. He invariably was in charge of the mobile bank at the Leicestershire Show each year and it was rumoured that, having balanced the cash and leaving the show, he tried to drive his Ford Anglia through the turnstiles, having over-imbibed with some of the visiting customers.

It was with Peter and two of his friends that I visited London for a trip to Wembley to see England play The Rest of the World. After the game it seemed a good idea to tour around the district of Soho to see the sights. At one establishment we made a hurried exit when we found out that 'near beer' was being served and demanded our money back. Much to our surprise, it was returned to us and we went on our way rejoicing. A pub crawl finished the evening off before we returned to our hotel exhausted and not a little inebriated.

There was a great social atmosphere at St. Martins and I found myself involved in playing table tennis for one of the bank teams. Several of the teams in the league played in social clubs and inevitably the bar was visited before playing. This was obviously a deliberate ploy by the opposition to ply us with liquor and hopefully affect our performance. In some cases it had the opposite effect and a couple of pints inspired us to play like demons. Golf was another of the pursuits which attracted me and after work, four of us made our way to the Leicester Municipal course, where we could play for the princely sum of three shillings and sixpence. Bowling alleys were very popular in the area and there were regular challenge matches between the banks, invariably won by the strong mixed Westminster team.

St. Martins was one of the largest provincial branches in the country, with around 90 members on the staff and totally different from the small branch at Grimsby. There was a quick turnover of staff and it was difficult to get to know everyone. There were one or two characters who had been there a long time and were nearing retirement, and one of these was the chief cashier, affectionately known as 'Davvy'. He was a law unto himself and would think nothing of putting his 'till closed' notice up at 2.30pm and having a nap on the counter. This was usually after a strong liquid lunch, to which he was very partial. The Manager knew all about this and accepted the fact that 'Davvy' was shortly to retire and was just a cross to bear until he went.

The Christmas parties were something else and very popular. Sandwiches and snacks were prepared by the female staff and beer and wine provided by the men. This all took place in the bank itself, which was a fairly old building with high ceilings, chandeliers wall lights set high up. I well remember later on when the party was progressing well that some bright spark decided to lob oranges into the cup shaped wall lights. And what went on in the basement where the strong room was located was nobody's business. I know that some members were disciplined and all future parties were held elsewhere in local hotels.

Leicester City Football Club had their account at the branch and each Saturday home game required volunteers to go to the match and collect the takings, return with the Securicor van and deposit the cash in the strongroom. There was never a shortage of volunteers and I made it once or twice and enjoyed the game from a reserved seat in the stand. The only snag was that we had to leave before full time to avoid the crowds, but it was a popular perk.

It was during my stay at Leicester that the age of computers had arrived, and the initial preparation was tedious and involved long hours of overtime, much appreciated by some members of the staff, eager and willing to volunteer to boost their income.

During my time at Leicester, I was involved in manning one of the sub-branches at Evington Road, an area populated by Indians and Pakistanis. It was here that I came face-to-face with the difficulties of understanding the various dialects, particularly when there were so many customers called Patel, the equivalent of the English Smith. Fortunately in those days there weren't the racial problems experienced at present and a peaceful atmosphere prevailed.

To broaden my experience, I was sent on relief to Belgrave branch and first met a character called Malcolm. We were on the counter together and in quiet periods, I was on the receiving end of a never-ending fund of jokes. Although Malcolm was some 12 years younger than me, we became firm friends, visiting each other's homes. In spite of transfers to other branches and my eventual resignation, we kept in touch and still visit each other to this day.

23. LOUGHBOROUGH

The end of my banking career

After a couple of years at St. Martins, I was transferred to Loughborough High Street branch, some 20 miles away. It was a pleasant drive through the Charnwood Forest area and it was during one of these journeys in the winter that I was involved in a slight accident with another car coming from the opposite direction. The roads were treacherous and a skid on a bend resulted in collision. Fortunately little damage was done and coincidentally the driver of the other car was a girl from Leicester branch, whom I knew from my days at the same office. After an exchange of details we went on our way with the usual words, "Fancy bumping into you."

Later on that year I had another argument with a herd of cows on one of the country roads. A farmhand was trying to manoeuvre a herd of cows from one field across the road into another. I had slowed down to allow them passage when a lone animal suddenly ran across in front of me and although I took evasive action, I was unable to avoid it. I hit it fair and square and it finished up over my bonnet and caught the roof before landing behind me. Fortunately it was unhurt but the farmer told me it was pregnant and I would probably be sued if it was unable to calf. My car was drivable and I arrived late at the bank explaining that I had had a mishap with a pregnant cow. They thought it was funny but I was not too pleased as I had to pay for the damage to the car. I heard later that the offending beast had borne fruit (a calf) and that was the last I heard about it.

The High Street branch was much smaller than Leicester with a Manager, Chief Clerk, and eight staff. The Chief Clerk was an inveterate smoker and he would call in at the local tobacconists to buy his 'nails' (coffin for the use of), as he called them. He eventually was transferred and his place was taken by an Irishman, divorced with five children. I never did find out how he coped with a large family, except that he had female assistance, as he put it. When he was taken ill, I, as the next senior member of staff, was asked to take over his position (promotion at last!). This of course was acting, unofficial and unpaid, and was the nearest I came to becoming a manager. I was not allowed to move house and the powers that be insisted that I made my own way there at my own expense every day. It was at this time that my account gradually became overdrawn and my name began to appear in the 'blue book' with the 'bad boys'. Eventually I was invited to Staff Department in Birmingham to explain myself as employees were not allowed to go into the red. The Staff Controller and I did not see eye to eye as I tried to explain that it was the bank's fault that I was spending my cash on petrol to get me to Loughborough and back. In addition the bank had automatically stopped my Large Town Allowance when I left Leicester. I was unhappy and left Staff Department with a warning ringing in my ears that I had to curtail my spending and 'pull my horns in.' I had put my account in order but was still unsettled and by mid-67 I had had enough, and after long and intense discussions with Joan, I decided to resign from the bank and return to Grimsby, after 26 years' service in the bank. No gold watch for me!

24. A FISHY BUSINESS

Something completely different

So, back home and out of a job. At around 40 years of age I had to find a way of keeping my wife in the manner to which she had become accustomed. Through my father-in-law I obtained a position as sales representative for a wholesale fish company. This involved learning the hard way with an early morning start at the fish market and absorbing all the intricacies of the fish trade. As an ex-banker I found this way of life totally different and was aware of an invisible barrier between myself and the long serving staff, most of whom had been in the fishing industry since leaving school.

Nevertheless I persevered and spent one week away visiting existing customers and drumming up new business, then the following week would be spent in the office or down at the fish dock. This one week on one week off became a regular routine and Joan gradually got used to the idea of my leaving on Monday morning and returning on Friday afternoon.

At the end of each week I had a discussion with the Managing Director outlining my progress and plans for attracting new business. Although I had been made a director of the firm, I felt that my position and promotion was resented and it was during one of these informal chats that I brought up the subject of the psychological barrier between myself and some of the staff.

During this time I was seconded to the Fish Cake factory where I had my own office and secretary. This proved to be a fascinating experience for me, particularly when there was a strike and I found myself involved in helping to make the products and pack them for deliveries, including samples of experimental flavoured cakes exported to the continent.

It had been an interesting insight of life in the fishing industry and had given me an opportunity to travel the country, meeting some rare characters, but I was beginning to realise that it wasn't really what I wanted out of life. After a year or so, I came to the conclusion that my position in the firm was untenable and still resented by some members of the staff, and I handed in my resignation.

Another two years older and out of work again. So it was back to family discussions and scanning the newspapers and situations vacant columns. It is said that, by the age of 40, one should be settled in a job for life, but over the years, attitudes have changed. I had an open mind but no qualifications, only 26 years' experience in the bank. Not only had I a wife to support, but two growing girls. So, on to the next chapter of my life.

25. LINCOLNSHIRE LIFE

Driving at Cadwell and Donington Park

More discussions with Joan resulted in my looking around for another job. One particular position that appealed to me was Advertisement Manager at the County Magazine, Lincolnshire Life. I decided to apply and was invited for interview with the owner, Roy Faiers. The offices of the magazine were located on the top floor of the Barclays Bank building on the main street and as well as Lincolnshire Life the suite of offices was the home of This England, a quarterly magazine with a circulation of 100,000 throughout the world. I was successful in my interview and was introduced to the staff, including the previous Ad Manager who showed me the ropes in his first week before leaving for pastures new.

One of my first jobs was to road test an Alfa Romeo in the nearby city of Lincoln. Now this was something I hadn't bargained for, but apparently it was a question of doubling up on tasks to be done as the editor was also the art editor. Obviously this was done for economic reasons and I was enthusiastic about the unexpected sideline as I was a keen driver. In my second week I shot off to Lincoln to the Alfa dealer and was delighted to be told that I could have the car for the day. This was bliss and I thought to myself, *What an excellent way to start a new job.* The only problem was that the dealer expected quite naturally that a write-up would appear in the magazine, and as this was completely new ground for me, I was somewhat concerned. So I took the car, enjoyed the drive and worried about the write up later. After a labour of love, the write-up appeared in the following month's issue and I heard no disparaging remarks, so I thought, *This isn't so bad after all.* My main job of course was to sell advertising, and soon I was touring the county visiting would-be advertisers. All in all, they were a pleasant lot apart from one or two aggressive, outspoken car dealers who told me in no uncertain manner to get lost. Gradually, I developed another layer of skin and began to enjoy meeting people from all walks of life and found that it was relatively easy to sell advertising, even though it was a slow, painstaking job, unlike the high pressure selling techniques of the daily newspaper reps.

The ad copy was dealt with by the Production Manager, Mr. Box, a true gentleman, one of the old school, who had moved up from the south of England where he had a senior position on one of the local papers. He was instrumental in teaching me the mysteries and technical terms of the printing industry, for which I was forever grateful. He always addressed me as 'Mister' and was a man of strong views on discipline and respect. I got on well with him and was amused one day to see him coming out of the editor's office, red in the face with his moustache bristling. Apparently he had been chasing the editor for copy which was not forthcoming. It was always the same at the end of each month when all advertising and editorial copy had to be taken down to the printers, some 70 miles away. Only with a lot of cajoling and threats was the magazine produced each month on time. I had been under the impression that any publication carried a large staff and was surprised that it was possible to produce a monthly issue with a handful of people.

After a couple of years the publication of This England was transferred to Cheltenham and the offices sold. This meant that Lincolnshire Life had to find another home and I was given the job of finding alternative office premises. It was a traumatic move and I was relieved to settle in a private house converted to offices in Dudley Street, where I was in charge of just three staff and a part-time editor. As I was responsible for putting the magazine together with the editor, I had to take on part-time ad sales reps in different parts of the county. The magazine was printed at Warners of Bourne in South Lincolnshire and before the end of each month, the Editor and Production Manager would make the two hour trip to 'put the issue to bed.'

I did have an approach from a printer in Cambridgeshire to print the magazine and he arranged to fly himself up to Lincolnshire to talk things over. His offer was cheaper than my existing printer and he offered to fly me and the editor down to his printworks to cast an eye over his equipment. It was a blustery day and the editor declined, saying he would rather drive there. We took off from Kirmington in his Cessna and after a very rough trip, alighted on a temporary landing strip near the printworks. We did a tour of inspection, had lunch, and the editor drove back whilst I had to endure another flight in squally conditions. Was I pleased to see the airfield at Kirmington?! After a long discussion we decided against the change of printers and carried on with Warners.

The Printer's Cessna

It was quite a regular thing to be approached by different printers and another such offer came from Roger Bowskill in Exeter, and the same procedure was adopted as before, except that Roger didn't own a plane and it was a long trek down to Devon. I was impressed with the setup and the terms of the offer and decided to accept. So Lincolnshire Life was then printed some 300 miles from home. He also printed the calendars for a number of years. Due to the distance involved, the monthly proof reading and final checks were all carried out by post and, postal strikes excepted, it seemed to work pretty well. We made an annual trip down to Devon where we were made welcome and royally entertained by Roger and his wife.

I was confined to the office more and more, much to my dismay, with the occasional foray to see regular advertisers and keep them sweet. From time to time, the morning post contained intriguing invitations to the launch of a new car, the opening of a new hotel or shop, together with other fascinating offers such as attending the opening of a new Golf Course in Sweden. I jumped at the chance to wear another hat as the Holiday Correspondent or Sports Editor, as well as Motoring Correspondent. The Swedish trip was only for three days and included a visit to the golf course on the outskirts of Gothenburg, a sightseeing trip and a visit to a night club in Gothenburg. The journey was made by sea from Immingham to Gothenburg, and the trip across the North Sea was rough but otherwise entertaining. In the Press party there were several other journalists from sporting magazines and national newspapers and it gave me an insight into how the real correspondents went about their business. Obviously I was not a qualified journalist or a union member and it was an interesting experience.

Back in the office and down to earth once more, I browsed through the mail with a certain lack of enthusiasm, until I came across a letter from an agency in London, inviting me to an adventure weekend. There was an exciting choice of free-fall parachuting, abseiling, white water rafting, potholing or motor racing. I decided on the parachuting but this proved to be too popular and all positions had been taken on the course, so I went for the motor racing. This took place at Cadwell Park, near Louth and involved a day's instruction on Formula Ford racing cars, followed by a free night's accommodation at the Golf Hotel in nearby Woodhall Spa. The cars were single seaters and unfortunately governed so that speeds in excess of 100mph were unobtainable. This was probably a good idea as a safety measure as there is usually at least one mad-head on these courses. It proved to be an exciting afternoon and certificates were handed out to the participants at the end of the day. Then followed a dinner and celebrations at the hotel to finalise an adventurous weekend.

One of the perks of being in the publishing business, is the number of invitations to all manner of events and functions. One of the more exciting letters in the post was from Gordon Lamb, the Porsche dealers in Chesterfield, on the occasion of an open test day. A number of their important customers had been invited to take their own cars to Donington Park Race Circuit for a series of events including manoeuvrability tests, hand-brake turns, quickest lap times, etc. I was invited, but not being affluent enough to own my own Porsche, they were kind enough to supply me with a 928 for the day. This was an exhilarating experience but sad to say my name did not appear in the winners list.

Formula Ford at Cadwell Park

Donington Park 1989

There were several cars on display, including a Rolls Royce with the number plate R1. This must have been worth a small fortune, as was the car next to it shown above, with the registration A1.

On another occasion we had a Dutch family staying with us when I was invited to a Ferrari open day at Donington Park. We had previously met them on an exchange visit with the Orpheus Choir and Jan Verschoof was the treasurer of the Nijmegen Choir. The father and son were delighted when I asked them if they would like to go with me. I was allowed to take one of them with me on the track, but trying to impress, I spun off at speed on one of the sharp bends, finishing up backwards against a fence. Luckily no damage was done and we continued at a more sedate pace. Later there were demonstrations by experienced Ferrari drivers, showing just how it should be done.

26. NORWAY

An icy visit to Oslo

I had the opportunity to visit Norway with my wife in connection with one of our major advertisers. We had only briefly been there over the border from Sweden and it seemed an ideal opportunity to see a little more of the country. It was during winter as we left from Heathrow to land on a snow-covered runway at Bergen, en route to our final destination of Oslo. The break was only a few days' duration and we settled in at a hotel in Oslo to make plans for where to go and what to do. Judging by the thick snow and icy conditions it would seem that we would not be going very far afield. The hotel was comfortable with a huge log burning fire in the centre of the main lounge and it was a delight to return to this after a trip to the shops. The pavements were kept clear by means of underground electric heating, so there was no problem of walking through slush.

Our list of places to visit was limited by weather conditions and we confined ourselves to trips to the theatre, museums and of course, reluctantly as far as I was concerned, the shops. One day it was so bitterly cold that we decided to go to church and found ourselves sitting next to a Norwegian who spoke excellent English. He was most helpful and much to our surprise he told us that King Haakon was in the church on the upper balcony. So we were in good company! Obviously we didn't understand what was going on but at least it was a haven of peace and warmth from the elements. As far as the hymn singing was concerned, we just tried to follow as best we could by watching other people's mouths. It was an intriguing experience and our new friend was kind enough to give us information and advice about the city and suggested one or two venues.

This trip was not a holiday as such so we were unable to extend our visit to include the fjords, which we had hoped to go to. Something to look forward to in the future. It had been a short but interesting visit, but we were glad to get back home where it was not quite so wintry.

27. SPANISH PROPERTY FORAY

Potential UK property agents

With a view to improving my financial situation, I decided to look around for something to bolster my income, which could be done on a part-time basis in conjunction with running Lincolnshire Life. Being a sun-worshipper, I contacted a company which was selling properties in Spain, with a view to becoming an agent and advertising them in Lincolnshire Life. This involved a short training course and a visit to Torremolinos, where the company was based.

Joan was not too keen on the idea as she thought that it was just an excuse to have a short holiday in the sun. How could she think this when all I was trying to do was to improve our finances? Anyway, on this occasion, I, as the breadwinner, got my way and, together with six other would-be agents, flew to Spain to stay in a luxurious hotel where we met the Chief Executive who was a German. He spoke perfect English but had this strange idea that we should all be in bed by eleven o'clock at the latest so that we should be fresh and bright the following morning.

He used to disappear at 10.30pm whilst we were still in the bar enjoying ourselves and even came down at 11pm to see whether or not we had retired. We may have incurred his wrath but there was no way that we were going to be dictated to by a German in our private lives, even though we were possibly going to work for his company in the future. However, he became resigned to our strange English ways and during the ensuing days we got along on a more friendly basis.

One of the agents from Yorkshire was an ex-pilot who

flew Lancasters during the war, and when he was asked quite innocently by the German if he had ever been to Germany before, he said that he had visited Berlin several times but his trips had only been of short duration. Long enough to drop a few bombs, but he didn't tell him! During seven days of exhausting trekking around in the hot sunshine and lectures in the hotel, we managed to fit in a little socialising and found that the 'boss' wasn't such a dry old stick in the mud as we had first thought.

We were shown some delightful properties, some only in the early stages of construction. Our cameras were working overtime, taking photos to add to our portfolio of brochures to show our potential buyers. At the end of the week we returned to England, armed with colourful literature and villa plans and designs and full of enthusiasm for selling on a part-time basis. Alas, with a full time job on the magazine, I found that I could not devote the time to it and my visions of generous commissions on sales faded.

When I arrived back home with a Mediterranean tan, Joan asked me if I had enjoyed my holiday whilst she had been looking after the children. When I said it had been a business trip, not a holiday, her reply was unprintable.

28. MOVE TO CHELTENHAM?

House viewing

Back down to earth again, devoting my time to increasing advertising sales and taking on part-time sales representatives throughout the county. This gave me more time for administration and producing a more attractive magazine. This was becoming even more important as two more county magazines had come on the scene and competition was increasing, particularly the selling of advertising space by aggressive sales reps from the competitors. By this time the owner of the magazine had moved to Cheltenham to more palatial premises for the headquarters of *'This England'*, a quarterly magazine devoted to England's 'green and pleasant land'.

In addition, he started other county publications covering the counties of Devon, Hampshire, Wessex, Sussex, Norfolk, and the Cotswolds. Eventually the group known as English Country Magazines comprised ten publications, covering mainly the south of England, with Lincolnshire Life the exception in the north. A head office was established in London and from time to time I went to meetings of the regional managers to compare policy and progress and develop new schemes to improve content and sales. In due course a position arose for a national sales director and I was offered the job and duly went down to Cheltenham with my family for a long weekend. During this period we scoured the area looking at suitable properties but houses were so much more expensive than back in Lincolnshire. I explained the situation to my boss who agreed my salary was insufficient to cover the increased cost of living in that area.

Various schemes were discussed, even the possibility of staying in Lincolnshire and keeping an eye on Lincolnshire Life, whilst travelling to Cheltenham for three or four days a week to run the magazine group. However, this proved impractical and in due course a new man was appointed to the position, a brash, aggressive advertising man from a newspaper group in south west England. His priority was to visit each area for a few days and improve methods of selling technique. When he came to see me, he accompanied me on my sales trips to introduce himself to the regular advertisers, but it was obvious from the start that there was a clash of personalities. This came to a head when we were given impossible sales targets and I was increasingly unhappy with the situation. As it happens, the position resolved itself as the new man only lasted six months and was then dismissed. The reason was partly due to his attitude and the fact that he decided to purchase an expensive car, at the company's expense of course, and charge extortionate travelling expenses.

So we were back to square one after an unsettling period.

29. TO BUY OR NOT TO BUY...?

A momentous decision

It was at this period that I had given a lot of thought to the future and after prolonged discussions with Joan, I wrote to the owner, offering to buy the magazine. The offer was taken up but the asking price was high and I went through a traumatic period in discussions with family, accountants, solicitors and my bank manager. In the end, a solution was reached and with the assistance of loans from the bank and other private loans, and with my house mortgaged to the bank, the final decision was taken and Joan and I became directors and owners of Lincolnshire Life, though not without a lot of heart-searching.

I persuaded Joan to work for me (cheap labour) and also my father-in-law to look after the accounts. Now that we were working for ourselves, the hours tended to be much longer and it was not uncommon for me to work Saturday mornings and quite often Sunday mornings. After four years of independence I was able to pay off the bank loan and settle down to making a living. It was hard going at first but gradually began to pay off and we were in a position to take the occasional holiday, though this proved difficult with such a small staff. Initially I used to telephone the office from Spain or wherever I was on holiday, but even if there had been a crisis, there wasn't a lot I could do about it so in due course we were able to go away and relax without a thought of what was happening back home.

In due course I advertised for part-time staff to sell advertising and took on ladies in different parts of the county. This was in the days when you could put an advertisement in the paper and specify what sex you required. My job was made easier as all I had to do was collate all the incoming ads and place them in appropriate positions in the magazine.

I approached David Robinson, who previously was a contributor to the magazine, to accept the position of part-time editor. This was an ideal situation as he had written books on Lincolnshire, had appeared on television and was an authority on Lincolnshire, as well as having many useful contacts throughout the county.

Our offices were centrally located in Dudley Street, Grimsby, where we occupied the upper floor of a house, the ground floor being let to an insurance company. Although we were situated in the north of the county, rather than in Lincoln or somewhere more geographically central, it seemed to work out quite well.

There were three good size rooms, one for the editor's use, one for subscriptions and advertising, and a private office for my use. And very importantly there was parking space at the rear. I would never have believed that a county magazine could operate successfully from such small premises with such a small staff.

30. THE RITZ

A weekend of luxury

From time to time the morning post would contain invitations and one of particular interest was a letter from the Ritz Hotel in London asking if I would like to spend a weekend at the Ritz with my wife or partner, obviously with the intention of giving them a write-up in the magazine. This was an opportunity to see how the other half lived and it took me all of five seconds to make a decision to go. Joan thought I was joking when I asked her if she would like a weekend at the Ritz. We took the early train, changing at Newark, where we sat on the platform eating sandwiches for breakfast. Not a very auspicious beginning to a weekend of luxury. Arriving by taxi at the Ritz, we were introduced to the Deputy Manager who took us on a tour of the hotel before showing us our room.

Overlooking Piccadilly, the suite comprised a spacious lounge with three piece suite and desk, a luxurious bathroom and toilet and bedroom with a huge double bed. On the mantelpiece was a bottle of special Ritz pink champagne with a note instructing us to ring the bell for service when we were ready to sample the drink. A sudden thirst developed, the buzzer was pressed, and within five minutes of arriving, we were sitting back in luxury savouring a glass of champagne each and saying, "This is the life." It was a pleasurable sensation to see how the other half lives and we were determined to make the most of it. Shortly afterwards, in mellow mood, I telephoned two friends who were staying in London for the weekend and invited them over to share the bottle as there was no way that we would be able to finish it on our own. Lunch was taken out at a nearby restaurant and the four of us returned later to sample the traditional 'tea at the Ritz.' This was a popular occasion, with the stipulation that the ladies should wear hats and the gentlemen dressed smartly – no jeans and open-necked shirts here! For the princely sum of eight pounds we consumed tea and cakes – expensive but delicious. It was fascinating to look around and analyse people, picking out those who were on a one-off visit and those who went regularly as a way of life. After a delightful dinner and entertainment in the evening, our friends returned to their hotel and left Joan and I to wallow in the comforts of the Piccadilly suite. As a special treat we decided to have breakfast in the bedroom and duly telephoned our order from the extensive menu. Within a short time, a waiter arrived with a breakfast trolley and set it out on the table, leaving us with a pleasant smile and a murmured, *"Bon appetit."* With the inner man duly satisfied, we set out to explore London and all that it had to offer. A trip on the river took us past the old Humber Ferry, the *Tattershall Castle,* now in a permanent resting place as a riverside restaurant. Further down the river was the Flood Barrier, then regarded as one of London's spectacular sights. With such a wide variety of tours and entertainment, a weekend only gives you the opportunity to scratch the surface and after a hectic day we were pleased to return to the peace and tranquillity of the Ritz.

Sampling the pink champagne

In 1946 a young Irish lad, Michael Twomey, started as a luggage lift operator and he was still there as Head Waiter in the Palm Court. He was a most friendly and affable character, and typical of the staff with whom we came into contact. Many famous people have stayed there, including Sir Winston Churchill, de Gaulle, Eisenhower, Noel Coward, Charlie Chaplin and the Aga Khan – and now Joan and Geoff Lenthall!!

The following morning we made our way to the station and on the train heading north, we thought, what a way to celebrate a birthday or similar occasion. But for us it was back to reality and a return to the office to see what other interesting offers were in the post.

31. VALENCIA

Courtesy of the Spanish Tourist Board

Some weeks afterwards I received an invitation from the Spanish Tourist Board to visit Valencia for a few days, together with other journalists from newspapers and magazines. We all met at Heathrow where we were surprised to be taken to a twin-engine private plane just large enough to accommodate our party. The baggage was stacked at the back and everyone was warned that, as the only toilet was at the rear of the plane and was inaccessible, it would be prudent to remember this fact when availing ourselves of the free drinks stowed under the seats. Needless to say, by the end of the three hour journey, there were a few crossed legs and painful expressions. We landed at a small military airport on the Costa Blanca where we passed through a perfunctory customs check before being welcomed by Tourist Board representatives and taken to a luxury hotel outside Valencia, where we were entertained for the evening and given a briefing on what had been planned for us.

Various excursions included visits to museums, markets, property developments and a 'bodega.' The latter was the highlight of the trip, particularly for those who were wine drinkers as we were shown the whole production process from the crushing of the grapes to the finished article, which also included a tasting session. We came away somewhat woozy, clutching a presentation box containing three bottles of delicious Spanish Rioja wine. The days passed all too quickly and there was little time for relaxing in the glorious sunshine, except in the evenings when the hospitality was generous to say the least. There were a few thick heads on the return journey, but it had been an illuminating experience.

View from Javea

32. MINTEX ROAD TESTS

A day of driving and a night of boozing

As motoring correspondent I was invited to road test a variety of cars for local dealers and others further afield, followed by the usual write-up. One such invitation came from Gordon Lamb, the Porsche dealers in Chesterfield. There was no dealer in the Lincolnshire area and I was asked if I would road test the 924, 928, and 911. The cars were tested over a period of a week and there were a few odd looks as I parked the different cars in the drive after each session. An enjoyable experience giving an insight as to how the other half lives. When the Ford Fiesta was launched in London I was invited and after the launch at one of the top hotels, the speaker was Frank Muir, who I was delighted to meet, with the excuse of getting his autograph for my daughters. On the occasions when I was unable to carry out a road test for the magazine, I contacted an agency in London which would supply reports on any car, at a price of course. Looking back at some of the old magazines I came across a write-up on a BMW by a much younger and not so well known Jeremy Clarkson. He has come a long way since those days.

The highlight of the year was the weekend at Sherburn-in-Elmet where Mintex, the manufacturers of clutch and brake linings, held their annual event to give journalists the opportunity to test up to 70 different makes of cars on their testing ground. The location was an old wartime airfield, where runways had been converted into an oval track with S-bends, chicanes, and a high-speed straight. As motoring correspondent for Lincolnshire Life, I was invited each year with journalists from newspapers, motoring magazines, radio and television, to put the cars through their paces. The cars involved included models from the modest Mini to the regal Rolls Royce. All the drivers were subjected to a briefing before being issued with identity discs with photographs. It was all highly organised and before entering the track area the IDs were closely scrutinised by marshals. We were told that it was not a race track, but it was obvious that this instruction was not strictly adhered to as some of the high powered cars were driven to their limits. It was an exciting experience and one could imagine what it would feel like to be in a real competitive race. This was the nearest I got to realising one of my early dreams of becoming a Formula One racing driver! Naturally there were several hairy moments when inexperience resulted in spinning off the track or leaving it too late to brake when approaching a bend.

Bryan and I with the Rolls Royce

There were certain cars which we were not allowed to drive on the track and two of these were the Rolls Royce and the Aston Martin. Instead, a seven mile course on the open road specially marked for the occasion was used to road test these vehicles. The surprising thing was that on some occasions it was possible to just jump in the chosen numbered car and drive away, as there was no one there to brief you. This resulted in a few hilarious occasions when pressing the wrong buttons, opening the sliding roof instead of switching on the windscreen wipers, or other similar incorrect decisions. Part of the airfield was set aside to make a special rough track for testing the four wheel drive vehicles. This was great fun, particularly the 45 degree climb and drop, followed by the water splash.

Mintex 1987

It was not only journalists who were invited to this event but also well-known personalities such as Derek Bell, the Porsche driver and Noel Edmonds, the TV personality, who at that time was involved in saloon car racing. I elected to go round the track with him in a modified, souped up Ford Cortina and he showed me just how it should be done. There was a marquee for lunch, provided by a professional catering company, and a beer tent for those who were not driving. The day's activities finished around 5pm when a much needed shower was taken before the evening's event took place in a nearby hotel. This was when we could relax and let our hair down and on occasions I had taken a friend Bryan with me, and we spent a merry evening eating goulash or whatever was on offer and taking advantage of free beer. A fascinating experience and a great opportunity to try out such a variety of cars in one day.

33. CRANWELL REVISITED

A return to Cranwell to see the Queen

One of the many invitations received was from the Officer Commanding Royal Air Force College at Cranwell. This was on the occasion of the anniversary of the Battle of Britain and held in September each year. This time the event took place in the College buildings, not across the road where I had taken my ITW Refresher Course some years ago. After checking in at the guard house we were directed to the car park adjacent to the Officers' Mess, where we were introduced to our host for the evening. On this occasion it was a Lieutenant Colonel in the United States Air Force.

He was on a course at Cranwell and together with his charming wife, we were then introduced to the CO and his wife and offered champagne and canapés. Our host Gary was a bombardier and had flown many missions in B-29s, and the row of medals on his uniform was an indication of service in several theatres of war. Most of the people invited were either mayors of towns in Lincolnshire or dignitaries from other spheres. Don't know in which category we were!

Gary and his wife were excellent hosts and made sure that we circulated and met up with their acquaintances, as well as topping up our glasses. Throughout the evening the College Band was playing music to fit the occasion. As a finale everyone went outside to witness the playing of the Last Post and the lowering of the standard. It was a great evening and we are still in touch with Gary and his wife. Subsequently we met at the Eastgate Hotel in Lincoln, where we were introduced to Gary's mother, a dear soul who asked Joan to keep in touch when she returned to the States. As we hadn't blotted our copybooks by drinking too much champagne, we were fortunate to receive invitations each year.

Cranwell College

On another occasion the editor and I were invited to the anniversary of the Queen's birthday, which was a splendid event, with fly pasts and a banquet. Needless to say, security was very strict, with armed guards and plain clothes men everywhere. There was also a question of mistaken identity when it was discovered that in fact the invitation went to the then owner Roy Faiers, so we were kept under close scrutiny all the time, as Colin Carr and I were supposed to be the owner and his wife!

34. CRUISE

Around the Mediterranean

Although selling advertising was something comparatively new to me, I found that I was doing reasonably well and in due course achieved one of my ambitions to be top salesman in the group. This came at a time when Joan and I were longing for a holiday as we had only managed to snatch the odd few days. The prize was a cruise around the Mediterranean on a Greek ship owned by the Ellinis Line and by paying a little extra, we were able to take the girls, who were now teenagers. They were over the moon when I told them the good news and of course this meant a trip to the shops to buy new clothes for a life on the ocean wave. The duration of the cruise was only one week and we flew from Heathrow to Nice, to catch a coach to Cannes, where the Ellinis was moored. The cabins were luxurious and after unpacking and settling down, we proceeded to explore before returning to the top deck to watch the French coast gradually disappearing as the ship made its way to the first port of call at Barcelona, where there was time for a brief sightseeing tour before returning to the ship. Next stop was Palma, where the girls were whistled at by a group of policemen on motorcycles. We would like to have stayed longer on this delightful island, but our on-shore time was limited.

Tunisia was our next port of call and as the ship approached the docking area we were fascinated to see several locals gathered on the quayside with colourful stalls selling souvenirs. We had to fight our way through them to make our way inland to see the sights and of course the shopping centre. One of the local boys took a fancy to the girls and offered, in broken English, to be our guide and direct us to the bargain shops. No doubt he was working on a commission basis. We declined his offer but he was very persistent and attached himself to our party. We bought a few knick-knacks, including a bongo drum, which caught my eye. It now resides in the roof space gathering dust. After a couple of tiring hours we said farewell to our guide and returned to the ship.

The 'Ellinis'

After a short stop in Sicily, the cruise continued on to the port of Naples, where we had a longer stay. As we approached the harbour we were intrigued to see the massive American aircraft carrier, the U.S.S. *John F. Kennedy*. After disembarking with a Yorkshire couple we had befriended, we were standing on the quayside admiring the ship when we saw a group of American servicemen. They noticed our interest and one of them came over to talk to us. He was tall and handsome and the girls were thrilled when he said he was a pilot from the *JFK* and during the conversation we asked if it would be possible to have a look around the carrier. He told us there would be no problem and if we returned in one hour he would collect security passes and take us aboard. Excited at the prospect, we awaited the return of the ship's tender, used for taking the crew members ashore. It was only a short journey in choppy water and as we approached we realised just how enormous the aircraft carrier was. The tender tied up alongside the carrier and we were helped on to a platform, where a ladder led up to the entrance. A tricky business this turned out to be. Once inside we were taken first of all by Peter the pilot, to the bridge, where there was a magnificent view of Naples. Most of the crew must have gone on shore leave as the ship was virtually deserted and we had the opportunity to sit in the captain's chair on the bridge. From there we were taken around the seventeen decks, one of them big enough for a baseball arena. Peter took us to see his plane before leaving and we left after taking many photographs, saying a grateful farewell to our gracious host. The girls had taken a fancy to the immaculately dressed officers on board and Lindsay, approaching 17, exchanged addresses with Peter and they continued to correspond for some time. He had made a comment concerning the cross which Lindsay was wearing on a chain around her neck. He wanted to know if it had any particular religious significance. We found out later through correspondence with Lindsay that he had left the US Navy and joined a religious organisation. It seemed that he couldn't reconcile his life as a pilot and being responsible for the deaths of other people, with his new found beliefs.

In between the different ports of call we were able to enjoy the facilities on board, in the pool, casino, cinema and the first class entertainment each evening. Coping with three full meals a day was not easy, but we managed them, albeit suffering from excess weight at the end of the voyage. The highlight was the Captain's cocktail party when everyone dressed up for the occasion. This we nearly missed, due to the fact that one of my daughters, who shall be nameless, delayed us by not being ready at the time specified.

It was interesting to witness the smartly dressed ship's officers flirting with Lindsay and Carol and trying to persuade them to go to their cabins. Not only were my daughters approached, but my wife Joan received a similar invitation at the bar by one of the officers. No one asked me!

Even though it was only one week at sea, we had crammed a lot into it and seen many fascinating places, the highlight being the visit to the aircraft carrier S.S. *John F. Kennedy* and the tour of the ship. Finally, our last port of call was Genoa before returning to Cannes and a return to England.

35. MEETING MEG AND BENNY

Guests at opening ceremony

Chatting to Meg

The Four Seasons Hotel on the way to Lincoln was in the process of extending its premises with additional accommodation and we were invited to go for lunch and have a conducted tour. As an added attraction two special guests had been invited to speak after the meal. Those who watch television regularly will remember *Crossroads* and the stars Meg and Benny.

In those days we had to admit that we watched it but later it began to pall and our soap watching days were over. Benny was smartly dressed and was virtually unrecognisable and Meg was dressed in the height of fashion. They spoke individually about the show with amusing anecdotes and later we had a chance to talk to them. Meg had come in her Rolls Royce with personalised number plates NG 10 and I took a photo for publication in the Magazine.

I was beginning to realise that being in the publishing business did have certain advantages and was far more interesting than working in a bank. The only perk in the banking world was the fact that on our house loan we were only charged an interest rate of two and a half per cent, which in those days was I suppose quite a considerable advantage.

36. CONCORDE

Heathrow to Kirmington – a quick trip

It was a sad day for British aviation when it was announced that Concorde was to make its final flight at the end of 2003. For people living near a major airport the sight of Concorde was a regular occurrence but for those living in Lincolnshire it was a one off event when in 1993 this beautiful machine landed at Humberside airport, the ex-RAF bomber station of Kirmington. Flights were offered to and from Heathrow and we decided to take the coach down to Heathrow, stay the night in a hotel and fly back to Humberside in Concorde.

Concorde at Humberside Airport
Photo by David Lee

A group of some 100 passengers boarded the plane and relaxed in comfort to enjoy the flight. For most of us it was our first trip in this magnificent aircraft and at the prices charged, it would probably be the last.

It was well worth it for the experience of travelling so smoothly through the air at speeds in excess of the normal charter flights which we were used to. On this occasion we did not break the sound barrier as this was a separate trip over the North Sea and back. And it cost more too! It seemed only a short time after take-off when it was announced that we should shortly be landing back in Lincolnshire. However there was time to have a glass of champagne before we touched down on terra firma. How glad we were that we had taken the opportunity to fly in this, the ultimate in aircraft design throughout the world. We shall never see its like again.

37. MOSQUES, MUSLIMS, BANGERS AND BEANZ

A trip to Abu Dhabi

An opportunity to visit my son-in-law in the Middle East back in 1986, conjured up visions of unremitting sunshine, desert safaris, camels, Arabs, oilrigs, and endless vistas of sand dunes. Yes, they were all there in abundance, but what an eye-opener as we approached the airport at Abu Dhabi, to see a modern city with high-rise buildings, outstandingly beautiful mosques and well planned roads.

Much to my wife and daughter's dismay, I had booked our flight with Aeroflot – well, it was considerably cheaper for a start, although it involved an overnight stop in Moscow and touchdowns en route at Larnaca and Kuwait. The first leg to Moscow in a four-engined Ilyusin took around three hours. It was comfortable, the food was average (didn't care for the caviar!) and the service not very friendly.

We had a long wait at the airport before being taken to a transit hotel just outside the airport. It was a dismal-looking place best described as basic, and having booked in we went to the restaurant for a meal, also basic. One of our party, a lively Canadian, went to the bar and bought a bottle of champagne and offered to share it with us. This certainly enlivened the atmosphere and as we were eating we couldn't believe our eyes when we saw an armed Russian soldier standing behind a pillar, keeping an eye on us. We raised our glasses to him but he was not amused. The meal finished, we decided that we would like to visit the city and see the sights. Our attempts to leave the hotel were in vain as there was another soldier on guard at the exit and he refused to let us out. So there we were, effectively imprisoned in a hotel for the night. One would think that the war was still on. Well I suppose it was in the days of the Cold War. What an unfriendly lot the Russians were. And they don't even speak English! Reluctantly, we all made our way to our respective bedrooms, escorted by our guard with rifle. On reaching our floor we were handed over to a sombre-looking 'landing lady' who showed us to our room. The following morning after a light breakfast (no eggs, bacon and tomato here) we were escorted to the coach and as I looked back at the hotel which was virtually enveloped in a morning mist, I was reminded of a prison camp. I attempted to take a photograph of the guard who was at the top of the steps and boarded the coach. Suddenly he dashed down to the coach shouting and gesticulating and pointing to my camera. I just smiled, said, "Good morning," and packed my camera away. He then disappeared, muttering under his breath.

Joan and Lindsay on the Ilyusin

132

Our flight was delayed, owing to fog, and we visited the airport restaurant for a coffee to pass the time away. When the call came we boarded the aircraft and only then realised that my wife had left her anorak in the restaurant. I had a word with the stewardess, who fortunately spoke English and she allowed me to leave the aircraft, but I was stopped by two armed soldiers who refused to let me go any further. It was only after a walkie-talkie conversation with the stewardess that I was allowed on my way. But not alone, as I was escorted by the guards to the restaurant, picked up the anorak and returned to the aircraft. I had the feeling that I was a criminal – it was like being on a 'fizzer' again. After encountering a few dirty looks from the passengers who had been delayed further by my absence, I thanked the stewardess and settled down with my wife awaiting take-off. From the Russian capital we flew in a Tupolev – smaller, but lots of spare seats, so I was able to stretch out over three seats and smoke a cigar with my wine after the meal (couldn't do that now). Surprisingly I was allowed to visit the cockpit and chat to the pilot.

The airport at Abu Dhabi must be one of the most beautiful in the world and a real pleasure to spend the time as we waited for my son-in-law to pick us up and take us to his apartment. Abu Dhabi is an island about ten miles long by seven miles wide and is linked to the mainland by two bridges carrying modern dual carriageways to Al Ain and Dubai.

The apartment is only ten minutes' drive to the beach, but what a hair-raising experience it was as most of the locals drove like Michael Schumacher and accidents were frequent. The beach was out of this world with clean white sands, palm trees planted and watered by a complex system of piping, and a warm blue sea gently lapping the shore. As it was not a commercial resort, we had the beach to ourselves, apart from the odd local wishing to try out his English or study the female anatomy. No transistors, no one trying to sell time-share. Just a peaceful, idyllic existence, sunning ourselves, swimming, eating and drinking (but no alcohol!) In the afternoon we were joined by our son-in-law, who worked from 7am to 2pm. As he greeted us, he said with a smile, "It's tough in the Gulf," a phrase commonly used by the Brits working there.

Mosque at Al Ain

Lindsay and Joan on a deserted beach

Much to our surprise, there was quite a hectic social life in the city, with something to suit most of the 10,000 Europeans living and working there. Eating out was a multinational experience with restaurants offering traditional Lebanese, Chinese, Indian, Italian, and many other foods. We just had to have 'bangers, beans and chips' with a pint of lager for about £4 at the Red Lion, but we paid a little more for a special Seafood Evening which cost us £25 each! Only the hotel restaurants were licensed and alcoholic drinks were only available at the liquor stores, where the ration was £50 per month. Islamic laws were very strict and drinking and driving carried a heavy penalty, usually imprisonment.

Christian churches are represented, but naturally the picturesque mosques were everywhere – we could see more than 20 from our apartment window, as well as one of the magnificent Presidential palaces. Worshippers were called for prayer five times a day, commencing at dawn and ending at nightfall. We didn't need an alarm clock to wake us up!

View of Dubai

There was no shortage of Banks but we found one where an immediate withdrawal could be made without paying in any cash – the Abu Dhabi Blood Bank, where Steve and I donated a pint of good honest English blood in exchange for the equivalent of £40 each – not a bad deal and better than a cup of tea and a biscuit!

A weekend visit to Dubai was a must, where we stayed in the Hyatt Regency, a magnificent hotel with a revolving restaurant at the top, overlooking the coastline and city below. Also worth seeing was Al Ain, about 100 miles inland on dual carriageway all the way through the desert. Woe betide you if you hit a camel, for not only could it cause severe damage to the car, but you could be heavily fined. We had an overnight stop at the Jebel Ali Hotel, a beautiful complex with restaurants, swimming pools, tennis and squash courts. Golf, sailing, wind surfing and squash are popular with the British workers, whose salaries are attractive and tax-free.

Steve was employed by Adgas and we were fortunate enough to be able to use the company restaurant, which provided excellent food served by friendly Indian waiters. On one occasion we were all invited out by Steve's boss for a meal at one of the top vegetarian restaurants. We were offered a lift in his big Mercedes, complete with tinted windows, curtains and all the usual luxury extras. We were hoping that he might invite us round to his mini-palace afterwards, but apparently it is not the done thing out there.

Steve and his boss

Abu Dhabi is one of the richest countries in the world, where tourism was not particularly encouraged in those days, although package holidays are now available to this area. We were very impressed by the general cleanliness in the city, due in no small part to the army of labourers from Baluchistan, who could be seen every day packed like sardines on lorries on their way to work. The excellence of the road systems, the colourful flower-beds, trees and shrubs, picturesque fountains and beautiful Mosques were indelible images imprinted on our minds.

I am sure that England can learn a thing or two about administration of law and order, as we saw no indication of vandalism or graffiti. We could walk outside in the late evening without fear of being molested, which we dare not attempt in our home town. Crime was kept down to a minimum by the fear of severe punishment meted out to offenders. A pity we can't say the same about our country.

We look back on many happy memories of our visits to the United Arab Emirates, and look forward to returning in the future – God willing and health permitting.

38. CARIBBEAN CAPERS

Two laid back weeks in Jamaica

A late booking in January for a bargain package deal saw us winging our way across the Atlantic in a Boeing 757, heading for Jamaica with our neighbours Jean and Noel. Escaping from the English winter, we touched down in Bangor for refuelling, then headed south for the West Indies. After some 12 hours total flying time we landed at the 'Island in the Sun' in brilliant sunshine with temperatures in the 80s.

Neither of us had been before and our knowledge of the island was confined to Bob Marley and Reggae music, Harry Belafonte, rum and cricket. Jamaica is rich in cane sugar, beautiful flowers, lush greenery, mountains and waterfalls, and tourism is its biggest money-earner. It is not difficult to see why, with year round temperatures in the 70s and 80s, more or less constant sunshine and clean white beaches caressed the warm, blue Caribbean Sea.

When we arrived at the airport, we had no idea in which resort we would be staying, but we were lucky as we found ourselves booked in at the *Seawinds* complex in Montego Bay. It was a little off the beaten track but ideally situated for a quiet, relaxing holiday, with its own restaurants, swimming pools and private beaches, including a nudist beach for those wishing to achieve an all-over tan! Our rooms were on the 9th floor with superb views over the harbour and beaches, and we were able to see the visiting cruise ships, an impressive sight when lit overall at night.

Currency used in town was the US dollar and Jamaican dollar, but in the complex, 'Sharks Teeth' were the only legal tender (each worth one US dollar or 28 Jamaican dollars). It was confusing initially, but we soon got used to the idea, although it was a bit of a rip-off. In the restaurants it was more convenient to use credit cards.

Joan and I on the beach

The weather was hot and sunny with gentle breezes day after day and we spent a lot of time on the beach and in the warm sea. Trips were laid on to visit other parts of the island and entertainment organised every evening. Eating out in town at the many and varied restaurants was very reasonable on the whole and we just rang up from the hotel and a private car was sent to whisk us off to town and bring us back after our meal. We did slip up one evening when we booked at an

Italian restaurant 800 feet up in the hil
paying £30 each. That hurt! The only cor
a chat to the film star James Coburn and
were sitting at the next table. We spo
personal registration plate JC1, whi
shipped over for the duration of his stay.

Happy Hour

One of the most enjoyable tripe was to the Dunns River
Falls, near Ocho Rios. Everyone was issued with rubber
shoes and the idea was that our party of around 30 people
linked hands for safety and were escorted by an experienced
climber up the falls. We had been advised to dress in bathing
gear as it was a pretty wet operation. I had forgotten my
swimming trunks and had to borrow Joan's bikini bottom,
but no one noticed and Noel told me that it suited me! It was
something quite different and very refreshing.

As usually happens on holiday, the two weeks flew by and
we were soon on our way back, recalling happy memories of
the friendly, laid back people who never seemed to get out of

gear. But in that sort of climate, who wants to? It was to reality when the pilot informed us that it was freezing Manchester. Having had very little sleep, we were well ready for a rest on returning home, but still retained wonderful memories of this value for money holiday.

39. AUSTRALIA

Down under to see friends

Joan and I visited Australia for the second time in 1992 when we visited friends in Melbourne and stayed for five weeks. We flew by Singapore Airlines, with overnight stops in Singapore and Cairns, where we visited the Barrier Reef before touching down at Sydney. We were met at the airport by our friends Frank and Edith, who had driven up from Melbourne to Sydney, where we all stayed 10 days with their daughter and husband. During that time we covered most of the surrounding area including of course the Opera House, before moving off by car to Canberra, where we stayed for two days before leaving for the East Coast area by the 80 mile beach. Two more days at ex-neighbours of Frank and Edith, who had moved down to this delightful area. They owned a boat and took us out to a small island used for corporate holidays by companies whose personnel stayed in the luxury hotel and played golf, tennis or swum in the pools. There was also a small landing strip for light aircraft. It was here that we met our first kookaburras and brilliantly coloured parrots, which were tame enough to eat from our hands. After an idyllic time we pressed on to Melbourne to relax for a day or so before touring the vineyards, mountains and picturesque southern coastline.

Frank and Edith had lived near us in Park Avenue, Grimsby and had emigrated with their four daughters some years ago.

They had bought a large house in the suburbs of Melbourne and were able to accommodate us as well as their family. The girls had picked up the Australian accent but their parents still had a Lancashire accent with the odd Aussie slang thrown in. They had a planned itinerary, including trips to the Blue Mountains, the spectacular south coast trip, the vineyards and the Phillip peninsular to see the penguins, staying overnight in motels on the way.

Frank casting off

Sydney Harbour Bridge

He had a special place where he bought his wine and sherry and the two of us went to replenish stocks, returning two hours later. The reason for this was that the owner permitted customers to sample wines before they bought (what a good idea) and he was a busy man and just left us to it. Our wives realised what we had been up to when they saw our faces wreathed in smiles.

Frank had a Holden car and trailer and planned to take us to the outback for a few days, and what an experience that was. Living in such a vast country, distance means nothing to the Aussies and we travelled miles to the 90 mile beach, where they had bought a plot of land with the intention of building a holiday getaway place in the future. The sand was so hot that we had to run over the beach to reach the Tasman Sea. From there we headed inland to Lake Glenmaggie for a day or two sailing in his dinghy. We made camp on a plot of land he had bought in a nearby forest clearing. This was Joan's first experience of real camping and sleeping in a tent and she had mixed feelings. Frank, Edith and the dog slept in a large marquee and we had a small tent to ourselves with special candles to burn and keep the mosquitos at bay. A fire was started to roast the potatoes and we had a meal around the campfire to the accompaniment of a guitar. From time to time, Christmas beetles suddenly flew down, attracted by the fire, and strange noises could be heard from the surrounding forest.

In spite of everything we slept well and woke at dawn to another beautiful day. We were told that the Aussies love this sort of life, getting away from it all at weekends, and I must admit that we enjoyed it. I know that a lot of people in England like this way of life, but cannot guarantee the weather in their homeland.

It was extremely hot, in the 90s at the end of January, and the sheer vastness and open spaces in this magnificent country were overwhelming. In spite of rumours that 'Poms' were not generally liked by the Aussies, we found nothing but friendliness and acceptance by the natives who called a spade a spade. A fascinating country with so much to see and do and vast distances to travel. We would love to go again.

Koalas

40. DON'T MENTION THE WAR

The Lancaster at East Kirkby

In 1997 the Air Gunners Association invited a number of German ex-Luftwaffe fighter pilots to join them at East Kirkby, the home of the Lincolnshire Aviation Heritage Centre. It was a special day when the Lancaster NX611 was to perform a short taxi run and guests included Bill Reid VC and 'Jane', the 1940s pin up in the Daily Mirror. The occasion was to name the Lancaster 'Just Jane' and Mrs. Leighton-Porter (Jane) performed the ceremony, followed by a speech by Bill Reid. The BBC Television team were there to film the event which was broadcast on 'Look North'.

Frank, Geoff and Peter in front of 'Just Jane'

I had gone with two ex-RAF types, one of whom was a rear gunner in Lancasters, so we had some interesting conversations with some of the pilots in broken English and schoolboy German. For lunch we retired to a local pub for a 'gin and teutonic' (what else?). Later, the familiar crackling exhausts of the faithful Merlins were heard as the Lancaster taxied down the short runway. To finish off the day, the Lancaster from the Battle of Britain Memorial Flight thrilled the crowd with several low level runs over the airfield before returning to its base at Coningsby. This was a bonus for the 'old boys' and there were a few moist eyes.

41. ROTARY

Immingham Rotary Club

Through a member of the choir, I was invited to join the Immingham Rotary Club, which was in the process of being formed. Not being a 'committee man', I had my arm twisted and was persuaded to attend an inaugural meeting with three members of the choir at the Little London Hotel. With around 30 members, the club was formed and a Monday lunchtime venue at the Oaklands Hotel was set for weekly meetings. It wasn't long before I, with my experience in publishing, was approached to start a club newsletter on a quarterly basis. Some four years later I was asked if I would take on the publication of the District Newsletter, which involved gathering news from some 30 or so clubs. This was hard work, but enjoyable and similar to the job I was already doing. The main aim of the club was to support the community of Immingham in addition to other projects at home and abroad. At Christmas time some of us who had any singing experience visited the old people's homes in Immingham to entertain them with carols. Whether or not it was appreciated by the residents was difficult to tell, but they certainly looked after us at each place we visited, plying us with mince pies and drinks.

Fundraising for charities involved the organisation of events such as bonfire nights, golf matches, concerts, race nights and similar activities. Contacts were made with clubs abroad and twinning arrangements were set up, resulting in trips to Europe and return visits. A national Rotary cricket team was formed and Immingham were represented by no less than four members. A challenge match was arranged with a team from India and they had a successful tour in that country. Later, the Indian team visited the UK and we were involved in entertaining them for a few days. I well remember we organised a bit of a knees up at Keelby Village Hall and showed them some of our country dancing. They hadn't seen anything like it before and were highly amused. In all I was in Rotary for eight years, during which time I made many friends and it was with reluctance that I decided to resign to pursue other activities. In truth, in my later years in Rotary, I had retired and was finding that the production of the District and Club Newsletter was taking up a lot of my leisure time.

42. SWEDEN (1)

A free trip to Sweden

The Liseberg Loop

During my time with Rotary I was fortunate enough to win a prize in a raffle which was a weekend trip to Sweden on the *Tor Line* ferry from Immingham to Gothenburg. I made some enquiries and extended the trip to a week and took the car. This enabled Joan and I to visit Per and Gerd in Kungsbacka for a couple of days before exploring Sweden and taking a short trip across the border to Norway. Our daughter Carol had been in touch with a pen friend in

Sweden and they had already exchanged visits.

When Helena came to stay with us, she said that we must go over to meet her parents, Per and Gerd. They made us very welcome in their attractive home and of course spoke very good English, which was a blessing as our knowledge of the Swedish language was practically non-existent. We spent an exciting day at the Liseberg entertainment complex, sampling some of the nerve-tingling rides. We were impressed by the friendliness of the people and the beautiful scenery. We had been warned that there were strict laws about drinking and driving, even to carrying alcoholic drinks in the car, so our 'tippling times' were limited to the evenings.

After a couple of days we said our farewells and set off to see some of the countryside. We had pre-booked a hotel before we left England, and were able to book into our next destination at each hotel. An excellent system which worked very well. The Swedish countryside was very attractive, with good roads and many forests and lakes. Lay-bys were well in evidence, usually catering for the motorist by the addition of picnic areas with benches and tables. All very clean and well looked after. Whilst we were there we came across very little traffic and it was a real pleasure to cruise along at a steady speed, admiring the scenery.

It was only when we returned to Gothenberg that we met heavy traffic, and it was a nightmare negotiating our way through the city to the docks area where the ferry to Immingham was berthed. Having safely stowed away the car, we found our way to the bar for a well-earned rest and a drink. The crossing this time was relatively smooth and we enjoyed a good night's sleep before disembarking at Immingham and making our way home.

43. OMVC

Joining the Orpheus Male Voice Choir

I had been invited to join the local Male Voice Choir where my father-in-law was a member. Having been to several of the choir concerts and social functions, I had got to know some of the members and decided to join. They were a good crowd and the feeling of comradeship and fellowship was akin to the life in the services, with members from all walks of life. After a few years, in view of my previous banking background, I was asked to take over the position of treasurer and carried out these duties for nearly twenty years. Not only did the choir take part in festivals and concerts in England, but soon after joining we were invited to sing in Holland and Germany.

Many of the choir social activities took place at the old Ross Club (now sadly demolished) including barbecues and fund raising events. During this time I reached the age of 60 and together with my friend Bryan, who was 50 around the same time, we celebrated at the Ross Club with a '110 party.' All the choir members were invited, together with family and friends and it was a momentous occasion.

On previous visits to the renowned Blackpool Festival, the Orpheus had achieved second place on two occasions, singing under the baton of our musical director Arthur Robinson. Soon after joining, I was moved to the front row with my old mate Bryan and we had to know our music then – there was no miming as we used to do in the back row.

Arthur had been a singer in his own right and he had a rapport with men. He was able to paint a picture in words of just what he wanted and extract the subtle nuances and emotions that he felt himself. The joy of singing is evident as we sing the evocative strains of *Sunset Poem* by Dylan Thomas, the lilting *Myfanwy* or the full blooded *Gwahoddiad*, a Welsh hymn finishing with a resounding Amen. From a membership of nearly 70, the choir is now down to just over 50, mainly due to members moving away and the inevitable upward journey to join the celestial choir.

Bryan and I with the '110' cake

44. ORPHEUS TRIPS TO HOLLAND AND GERMANY

Our first trip abroad with the choir was to Holland and Germany and on the first occasion, wives were not invited, and some 40 members sailed across the North Sea to stay with members of the Dutch and German choirs, all in the cause of international friendship. The choir members embarked at Hull for the 22 hour journey across the North Sea to Rotterdam. After an evening meal on board, the lads retired to the bar area for a few beers and it was not long before we starting singing enthusiastically, and as audience reaction was good, they continued well into the night. One of the members was seen going round the audience in the bar collecting money in a battered old hat. What happened to this collection was never known but nevertheless the impromptu concert appeared to have been appreciated. Early morning saw the ship arriving in Rotterdam where they were met by the welcoming party from the Dutch choir.

We had already had an early breakfast and were well ready for lunch with our Dutch hosts en route to Nijmegen. The town had suffered heavily from fighting during the war, particularly the bitter struggle to defend the bridge over the River Waal. We were made very welcome at a local school where we were allocated to our hosts after a speech by their chairman and a glass of the local brew. Fortunately for us, most of our Dutch hosts could speak some English and we had no difficulties in making conversation. During our stay of four days we took part in a joint concert and as our final item we sang in Dutch a well-known song, which we had been practising for weeks. Not an easy language to learn. The response to this was a standing ovation. The rest of the time was spent sightseeing and socialising. Our host, Jan Verschoof, had been in the war, and during conversation he told us that he could forgive the Germans for invading their country but never forget. They were excellent hosts and on the day of our departure for Germany it was an emotional event with battle-scarred war veterans in tears. They appeared so grateful of the fact that the British had been instrumental in liberating their country from the Germans.

Setting off for the Continent

We had a long journey ahead of us as we made our way through Holland to the German border and beyond, skirting the Ruhr Valley before arriving in Meinerzhagen, situated in an area of lakes and forests. Any thoughts that may have been circulating in our minds about World War Two, were quickly dispelled as our ex-enemies unfurled a large Union Jack, waving it enthusiastically before greeting us and shaking hands at the pick-up point. The venue where we were to meet our hosts was a schoolroom, taken over specially for the event. A speech of welcome was made, followed by introductions to our hosts before girls in traditional costume circulated with drinks of Schnapps. What a way to start a holiday. It wasn't long before we were escorted to the homes of our hosts, Heinz and Hanna Voigt, for a welcome rest and meal and a chance to get to know each other. German vocabularies and phrase books were well in evidence and those who had difficulty in speaking German just shouted at their hosts in the mistaken belief that they would be understood in loud broken English. Living with a German family was an excellent way of learning the language although it must be said that quite a few of the hosts spoke some English. We Brits, being lazy, expect everyone to speak English, whatever part of the world we are in. Most of the German homes possessed their own private bar and after concerts, it was the practice to visit each other's homes and spend the rest of the evening and into the early hours drinking beer and schnapps, singing and cementing friendships – and trying to learn the language. In a typically thorough and meticulous German manner, they had arranged a trip on the River Rhine. It was a beautiful day as we boarded the boat with the skipper pointing out places of interest on the way. In fact he was quite a versatile chap and soon had us singing with him.

The beer and schnapps were flowing as quickly as the river and there was a round of applause from the other passengers after we gave an impromptu concert. As we passed the Lorelei on the way to the quaint little town of Linz, the sound of music and singing from our river cruiser echoed between the vineyard-covered hills on either side of the river.

One of the most memorable events took place on a beautiful summer afternoon, when both choirs, dressed in appropriate walking gear, climbed to the top of a hill overlooking the town. On the way, a rest was taken for refreshments before making our way to a log cabin at the top of the hill, where a hog was roasting on a spit. A German *oompah* band was playing and the bar was open. After sampling the fare and adding to their intake of alcohol, the air was soon alive with enthusiastic singing, which continued until the coach arrived to take us all back to our destinations.

The Germans certainly knew how to enjoy themselves and it was discovered that they did indeed have a sense of humour. The final concert was billed as an International Friendship concert and no one can deny that the aim was not achieved.

It was traditional for visiting choirs and their hosts to put on a show of some kind and plans were always kept secret until the actual performance. So after the concert we dressed up in our ballet outfits to perform a version of 'Swan Lake'. Twelve of us had been training for about six months under the watchful eye of a local ballet school mistress and the sight of twelve men of varying shapes and sizes prancing around in fish net tights and tutus brought the audience to their feet in a standing ovation.

'Swan Lake' swingers at rehearsal

On another occasion, six members of our social committee performed individual acts dressed as a farmer, milkmaid, tic-tac man, engineer, and footballer. I chose to dress up as a call girl, complete with fishnet tights, short skirt, high heels and a wig. I felt a right nerd up there on stage, but all the acts seemed to go down well. I didn't hear until the next day that I had caused an upset by using my host's name, Adolf, in my rhyme. He wasn't upset but another of their members with the same name had taken exception to my remarks as what I said had been a little too near the mark, as he was in fact having an affair at the time.

Later on, further visits were made to Nijmegen and Meinerzhagen, but sadly our hosts Jan Verschoof and Heinz Voigt had died and we were hosted by Jan and Els van den Brink in Holland and Heinz and Margo Schnepp in Germany. Heinz spoke very little English but his wife Margo had spent some time in England many years ago and her command of the English language was pretty good, though a little humorous at times. Hanna Voigt, the widow of Heinz, was learning English when we first visited and we still communicate each year – she writes in commendable English and I attempt to write in German, with the help of a dictionary of course.

Jan and Els van den Brink were excellent hosts and they and their two daughters spoke very good English. We had the impression that they were involved in wife swapping, so we were very cautious, particularly at bedtime after a hectic social evening. During one of the social evenings on the dance floor, 'Big Els', as she was known by the Orpheus members, had me in a very tight grip and one of the lads said she had me in a 'half nelson'. It certainly felt like it. When they visited us on a return visit, similar approaches were made at bedtime, but we made it clear that there was not going to be any 'hanky panky.' In spite of that, we remain friends.

Bryan, Mike and Geoff in drag

Links with the Dutch choir ceased when their membership increased to around 100 and we found it impossible to accommodate them all when they visited England. The opposite happened in Germany when the membership dwindled considerably and they were in danger of folding up.

Having lost two of our associations on the continent, we forged a link with a choir in Rauschendorf, near Konigswinter in Germany and exchanged visits with them on a regular basis. Our hosts were Adolf and Gisela Schmitz and it was fortunate that their two daughters spoke reasonable English. We had been very lucky with our hosts as on all occasions the hospitality had been very generous. During conversations we often used to say that the friendship links with choirs in Europe formed the basis for a solid international comradeship and understanding of each other's problems. Sadly, it was the politicians who did not see it our way, and inevitably some of us found ourselves staying in the homes of those whom we had been fighting against.

In spite of being our former foes, strong bonds of friendship were quickly formed and the war was rarely mentioned, except for the occasional question asking if their visitor served in the Armed Forces during the war. The general reaction was that the German people appeared to be apologetic for what happened – it was all in the past and predominantly the desire was for friendship and fellowship. This was certainly in evidence during the visits and nowhere could the hospitality have been more generous. Lasting friendships were made and still continue to this day. The visits, which were primarily planned for joint concerts, were a great success, as were the social events and the generous hospitality. Never was so much imbibed by so few in such a short time! Naturally, return visits to England were arranged. Since then, overseas links have been made with a choir in France and one in Sweden.

45. SWEDEN (2)

Another choir trip

With a view to extending the choir's boundaries, a choir from Sweden was invited to stay for a week and some two years later the Orpheus was invited to stay at Alingsas and join them in concert and social activities. After a nearly two hour flight, the plane landed at Landvetter Airport, Goteborg, where representatives from the Swedish choir took members to their home town of Alingsas. Hospitality was excellent and old friendships were renewed. Our hosts, Lennart and Ulla, lived in a beautiful house on the outskirts of town and offered us separate bedrooms should we so desire. They both spoke pretty good English and couldn't have done more for us.

Apart from a joint concert on the final day, barbecues, picnics, and visits to beauty spots dominated the visit, including a trip on an old steam train. It was interesting to note that the fireman/firewoman was in fact a woman. I wouldn't think there are many of those around. It brought back memories as we chugged along through the lakes and forests.

Plans were made for a journey to the picturesque fishing village of Fjallbacka, where we had a meal and visited a museum. On the way back we stopped by the Tjorn Bridge for a picnic before returning to Alingsas. Our hosts would not let us pay for anything as it was a reciprocal arrangement. A week of singing and socialising had taken its toll and it was a weary but happy choir that eventually went to the airport for sad farewells.

Fjällbacka

The flight home was enhanced (we think) by the choir singing 'Speed Your Journey' just after take-off. Judging by the applause from the passengers, it appeared to go down well. A long journey home by coach from Gatwick was the finale to an exciting and exhausting week in Sweden.

46. PONTYPOOL

Meeting our Welsh friends

The choir had heard that a Welsh choir, the Garndiffaith Gleemen, made annual visits to Spilsby in Lincolnshire, through a connection made by the local Methodist minister. It seemed a good idea to go and hear them, so a coach was duly hired and 50 choir members made their way to the market town and the church where the concert was to be held. As is the tradition with male voice choirs, we met up with them after the concert and joined them in a local pub for drinks and a sing song. We quickly made friends and as a result, we were invited down to their home town near Pontypool the following year.

This turned out to be a great trip and we received a welcome at the Pontypool Rugby Club together with glasses of beer to quench our thirsts after a long journey. What a start to the visit! Each member was allocated to a host for the overnight stay before preparing for the joint concert. My host, whose wife was the organist at a chapel, told me we would walk to the concert hall as it wasn't far, and we would call at his friend for a pre-concert snifter. Apparently they sing better with a drop of fluid inside them and boyo, was it strong? It was enough to make your eyes water.

The concert went well with a full house and we had carefully prepared as a surprise item at the end, a rendering of *Myfanwy*, sung in Welsh (we had a Welshman in our choir who had taught us phonetically). Although we received a standing ovation, we found out afterwards that the Pontypool area was mainly English speaking, but nevertheless it was warmly appreciated.

The Welsh love their singing and their rugby and years later we were able to invite the world famous Morriston Male Voice Choir to Grimsby to sing in the Central Hall. This was a tremendous occasion and there wasn't an empty seat. At the end of the concert, we were privileged to sing two joint numbers with the Morriston choir. Apparently this was a one off as they do not normally sing with other choirs, being the star performers. They also made some flattering comments regarding our choir which were greatly appreciated.

After the concert, as is the usual practice, an 'afterglow' social get-together was arranged when we were able to have a few drinks with our guests. They are very well known and have sung in most parts of the world, attracting full houses wherever they sing.

with Tom Jones and Shirley Bassey

One of the outstanding events in which the choir was able to take part, was a visit to Cardiff Arms Park, when the choir members and their wives had a weekend in Cardiff. The occasion was the World Choir concert, with nearly 10,000 male voices from all over the world taking part. Songs were sung in Welsh, English, and on one occasion in Russian when the combined choirs sang to the accompaniment of the Massed Guards Bands a rendering of the 1812 overture, complete with fireworks, cannon, and laser effects. This was a fantastic event and soloists included the evergreen Tom Jones who delighted the audience with, amongst others, *The Green Green Grass of Home*. A similar event was repeated the following year with the Royal Philharmonic Orchestra and guest artiste Shirley Bassey, who brought the house down with the ever popular *Hey Jude* and *Big Spender*. She was dressed in revealing slit skirt and the lads gave her a standing ovation after joining her in the chorus of *Hey Jude*. Other guest artistes included the BET Choirboy of the year, Oliver Sammons, and both events were conducted by Owain Arwel Hughes. The finale on both occasions was of course *'We'll Keep a Welcome'*.

Following the two successful concerts, a trip to the United States was organised on a similar basis, but a few problems arose which resulted in only around 6,000 choristers taking part in the concert in Atlanta. The next year, ambitious plans were made for another massed choirs' concert in South Africa and deposits were paid to the organiser. Unfortunately things went pear-shaped and the concert never took place. As a result, our choir lost £7,000 and other choirs throughout the country had similar losses. The organiser was sought by the Fraud Squad but he had skipped the country and disappeared. We had to put it down to experience.

In addition to having sung with the world famous Morriston Orpheus Choir, we also had the privilege of singing with the London Welsh Male Voice Choir. Both these occasions were memorable events. Several well-known soloists have performed with the choir and a full house is usually guaranteed when the Band of the RAF College Cranwell is invited. Other notable guests have been the Brighouse and Rastrick Band, the Black Dyke Mills Band and the Fairer Sax, a quartet of delightful saxophonists.

In 1997, it was with deep regret that I resigned from the choir on account of my hearing problem. I had been in the choir for some 25 years, had been Treasurer for 17 years and a Social Committee member for several years. It had become a way of life, not only the singing, but the social side and the fellowship with members from all walks of life. After seven years I have learned to accept it and live with it (or without it). Fortunately both Joan and I still attend concerts and social occasions. In addition I was appointed an Honorary Life Member and still retain close contact by virtue of my position as Editor of the quarterly newsletter, which I have been producing since 1996.

48. 9 SQUADRON REUNIONS

Finningley, Cranwell, Cottesmore

In addition to producing and selling magazines at Lincolnshire Life we sold various paperbacks dealing with the county and its people. The geographical location and general flatness of the county lent itself to the establishment of many airfields and it became known as Bomber County. For this reason I started buying in books about the RAF and the exploits of bomber crew members. One day someone came in to browse through our books and in conversation he introduced himself as 'Jeep' Jepson. He told me that he was an ex-rear gunner on Lancasters and his bomb aimer, who lived in London, had written a book about his time in the RAF, and perhaps I would be interested in selling it. I contacted him and arranged to sell his book and we became good friends. His name was Jim Brookbank and he was the founder member of 9 Squadron Association and invited me to become an Associate member with my wife.

Since then Joan and I have enjoyed reunions at Waddington, Cranwell, Cottesmore and Finningley, and it was fascinating to meet the old WW2 9 Squadron members together with the new boys who were stationed in Germany and flew over in their jets for the occasion. The reunions were held in the Officers' Mess, where they put on an excellent meal plus wines and spirits. These were happy occasions where the old boys mixed with the jet age youngsters and exchanged experiences and the inevitable line-shoots. Not only was Jim responsible for setting up the Association, he was Chairman, Treasurer and Editor of the magazine TABS (There's Always Bloody Something). Each year, weather permitting, arrangements were made for the

Battle of Britain Memorial Flight Lancaster to fly over before lunch to whet the appetites of those who had flown in them.

Many unsuccessful attempts had been made to sink the German battleship *Tirpitz*, by midget submarines and other methods and one of the subjects of discussion was inevitably the question of who was responsible for the eventual sinking. Was it the Lancasters of 9 Squadron or 617 Squadron? Part of the bulkhead which was recovered from the Norwegian fjord apparently bounced between the two squadrons until a neutral resting place was found. This good natured rivalry between the two squadrons carried on for some time.

At one of these reunions we found ourselves sitting next to an ex-RAF Flight Engineer and his wife, Don and Jean. After the meal and a few beers we found that we were getting on well and suggested meeting up again. They lived near Northampton and invited us to stay for a few days. This led to a close friendship and we exchange visits to this day.

49. MEMPHIS BELLE

The making of the film at Binbrook

People in the county of Lincolnshire will no doubt
remember this famous Boeing Flying Fortress when the film
of the same name was being made. Some of the flying scenes
were made at the old RAF Station of Binbrook, where one of
the bombers crashed in flames, but fortunately the crew
escaped. The production of the film required many ground
crew personnel as extras and an ad was placed in the local
paper for volunteers. There was an eager rush from
youngsters in the area to apply for the positions as they were
provided with uniforms and paid for their efforts. When I
heard that the filming was to take place at Binbrook, I

contacted Peter Cottam, a friend I had met through Lincolnshire Life. He had spent some time in America and because of his interest in aircraft, had been appointed UK representative of the United States Veterans Association, formed for the preservation of WWII military aircraft. They had even supplied him with a smart uniform and an honorary rank of Colonel. He was most interested and I contacted the publicity officer at Binbrook telling them of his status and we were given special entry tickets to visit at any time. This gave us the opportunity to see the film being made and to interview some of the actors and extras involved. Peter even got a few salutes from some of the local lads. Naturally, when the film was shown at the local cinema, we just had to see it.

The Grimsby Evening Telegraph each year organised a Literary Luncheon at the Winter Gardens and invited various authors to speak about their lives and the books they had written. Peter Cottam was invited, together with two other speakers and he arrived in uniform looking just like an American Colonel in the USAF. The only thing missing was the row of ribbons as Peter was just an honorary member of the Veterans Association, but he certainly looked the part.

During World War II, the Memphis Belle was amongst the first B-17s to complete its quota of 25 missions over Nazi-occupied territory without a member of its crew being killed. After recovery from a scrapyard it was sold to the city of Memphis and eventually flown to Memphis airport in 1946, where it rested for many years before being transported to its final resting place at Mud Island Airfield, which is managed by the Memphis Belle Memorial Association. It is there to this day as a friend of mine told me he had visited the site in the year 2000.

50. SINGAPORE

Bangkok, Malaysia and Indonesia

Our neighbour Noel Rees had worked at Conoco for many years and had obtained a position with Honeywell, which took him all over the world in connection with the oil industry. He had a two year spell in Singapore, during which time we looked after their house. Noel and his wife Jean had a two bedroom apartment in Singapore and invited us to go and stay with them. We had only briefly visited Singapore on an overnight stop to Australia and welcomed the invitation. We flew out with Singapore Airlines, where the charming Singaporean air hostesses looked after us so well and we were picked up by our friends at the airport.

A welcome meal awaited us at their apartment with a cool beer as the temperatures were in the high eighties with similar humidity. Unfortunately Noel was working some of the time, so the ladies went shopping whilst I visited a local hotel which had a gymnasium and pool. Noel would arrive home around five o'clock and make straight for the fridge for a beer. It was that sort of weather. When he took a few days off, we shot off by high speed ferry to the island of Bintan in Indonesia.

It was not a holiday resort and was by no means commercialised. The people were friendly but there was evidence of poverty in some areas. Our destination was the Royal Palace Hotel, which sounded very impressive. It wasn't five star, but luxurious and well-appointed, and we spent some hours by the pool with central bar. One strange thing was that when we asked for wine with our meal, we were told that it was only available at the nearby disco.

Our guide had suggested that we visit the nearby tiny island of Pulau Penyengat on a small boat. Apparently they don't see many visitors from England and we were surprised to see friendly, smiling children waving at us and following us down the streets. It was such a small island that we were able to walk around at our leisure. The locals made their living by fishing, which was presumably sufficient to keep the wolf from the door. We dread to think what their fate may have been when the *tsunami* struck in late 2004.

Back to Singapore, where we paid a night-time visit to the zoo. The following day we just had to see the fascinating Chinese quarter, where we spent some time before finishing the day with an excellent firework display. This was the first time that it had rained since we arrived. A trip to the riverside area to view the many shops and restaurants was next on the list, before returning to the apartment. We just had to pay a visit to the world famous Raffles Hotel, where we had a meal (naturally not in the expensive restaurant!) and a glass or two of the local brew and a *Singapore Sling*.

We had been told that we must visit the island of Sentosa, just off the coast. The journey was made by overhead cable car and the view from such a dizzying height was magnificent. It was worth the visit just to see the beautiful gardens and museum.

The next weekend we had a short visit to Malaysia before flying to Bangkok for a week. Noel was doing a few days of lecturing in the area and we booked in at hotel in the city, where we witnessed a typical Thai wedding and spent our time in the pool. The pollution in the streets was terrible and the traffic police had to wear masks to protect themselves. A trip to the floating market had been recommended and our taxi took nearly an hour to reach the river. This was quite usual as traffic congestion was appalling and the natives just seemed to accept it. On one occasion the driver of a car in front of us got out of his car and went for a coffee and was still back in time before the traffic moved on. When we did reach the river we boarded a high speed launch to take us to the floating market. This was an exciting experience as the boat skimmed through the water, which could hardly be described as clear or clean. There were all sorts of unmentionables floating around and we couldn't believe it when we saw a man from one of the riverside shacks cleaning his teeth in the water. By the time we reached the floating market, most of them had gone so we just had a quick look round and returned with Captain Birdseye, alias Michael Schumacher, at the helm. Certainly not to be recommended.

Once back on dry land with shaky legs we set out for the Royal Palace and temples which were incredibly beautiful, and we spent some time taking endless photographs. We were fortunate enough to have a chauffeur-driven car by courtesy of the company Noel worked for (one of the perks). He knew the area and was able to recommend places to see, which cut out a lot of hassle in finding our way around.

On the flight back to Singapore, much to our surprise, we were offered an upgrade to business class from economy.

This was the first time we had been lucky enough, so made the most of it for the three hour journey, relaxing in the luxurious reclining seats and sipping wine.

The three weeks we spent in Singapore seemed to pass so quickly and sadly we were soon heading back to England and freezing conditions.

51. SILHOUETTES

On stage with the Operatic Society

After being accepted as a member of the Grimsby Philharmonic Society and singing in the Messiah, I found that other concerts to be performed were a little on the heavy side for my tastes, and Joan suggested that I apply to join the Silhouettes, a local amateur operatic society. Joan and her father were already active members and as the company was looking for new blood, I decided to have a go. The mere thought of appearing on stage and acting and singing did not really appeal to me one little bit, but my arm was twisted and an audition was arranged with the Musical Director, Meg Lucas. They must have been desperate as, after singing up and down the scale a few times, I was in! At the time I was working at the Westminster Bank in St. Mary's Gate and the MD was a customer. I used to dread the day when she appeared as I was on the counter and she had a *fortissimo* voice and was quite outspoken. My first show was '*Merrie England*' and I must admit that it was great fun.

I quickly made many new friends and it was good that we both in it together, as normally we seemed to have different interests, though it didn't affect our married life. The banter and humour in the dressing room before the show, the smell of grease paint and the leg-pulling, all contributed to a happy atmosphere and the applause from the audience at the finale set the adrenalin flowing.

Our two children were still quite young so we had to do alternate shows, if we couldn't get a baby-minder, and this was a disappointment to us both. I well remember one of the shows 'Rose Marie', when I had chicken pox on the first night and missed the rest of the show. Fortunately no one else caught it and the show went on.

I was particularly thrilled to take part in 'Merrie England' when Joan took the part of the May Queen. It was my first show and it was with some trepidation that I took my place in the chorus, especially on the first Monday performance. By the time Saturday came around I was feeling more at home and enjoying it. After the final show on Saturday, it was traditional for all the cast to have a meal, when the President made a speech and presentations were made.

Joan as the 'May Queen'

52. VEE 1

Sixteen years old and going like a bomb

In my early days I was the proud owner of a Ford Anglia which I traded in for an Anglia Super 1200cc in 1963. The Ford franchise was owned by the Lincolnshire Motor Company and the Sales Manager was an old friend of mine, Vic Wells. Whilst looking round the showroom he mentioned that he was running a Cortina with registration number VEE 1. After some arm-twisting I said I would buy the Anglia on condition that he would re-register it with VEE 1. He eventually agreed but said that it would cost me five pounds to change the number. How times have changed. I have been asked several times of the significance of the number and my reply was usually that 'it goes like a bomb' (referring to the war days when the Germans were sending over the doodlebugs, known as the V1).

Whilst I was in the bank at Leicester I came across a large family company with several accounts in the name of Everard and it occurred to me that amongst the directors, there may be an individual with the Christian names of Victor Ernest or similar. Sadly there was no such name and my hopes of selling VEE 1 were in vain. I was subsequently approached by a local councillor who offered me £75 but I declined.

Over the years several offers were made to buy the number and I remember whilst I was parked at Kirmington airport, I was offered a measly £50 for it by the owner of a Rolls Royce parked nearby, who already owned VEE2. I declined and just transferred it each time I changed the car. It has been on my ancient Nissan 200 SX for ten years and is worth more than the car.

An approach was then made by a car registration company who dealt in purchase and sale of personalised plates and I eventually sold it in 2006 for £10,000. It was the best investment I have ever made.

53. BERLIN… AND BACK

A day's flight to the German capital

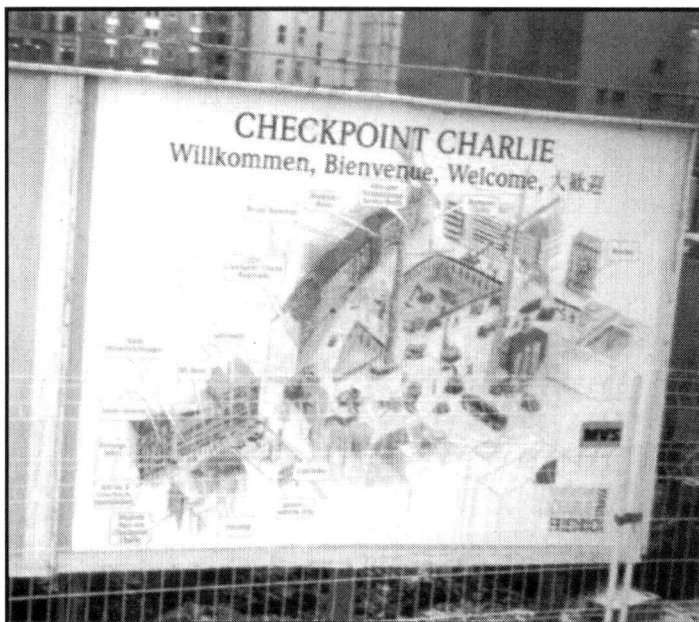

I was sitting with an old friend in the local pub talking about the good old days when he pointed out an ad in the newspaper he had been reading. His eyes moistened as he read it out to me. It said, "Day trip to Berlin." Harry had been an Air Gunner (Tail end Charlie) in Lancasters during WW2 and recalled the tragic consequences of his 13th operation when his aircraft was shot down on the outskirts of the German capital during a 1,000-bomber raid over 50 years ago. Sadly he was the only survivor and spent the rest of the war as a POW.

Joan at the Brandenburg Gate

The ad gave details of a day trip to Berlin by Airtours from Humberside airport. For old times' sake and to humour him, I said I would go with him accompanied by our wives, leaving at 7am from what used to be the old bomber station at Kirmington. It was different this time – no briefing, no Met report, no parachute or Mae West to carry out to the waiting Boeing 757.

Having had a hot breakfast over the North Sea, I suggested to Harry that he should test his guns. He smiled wryly and told me how different it was in his lonely rear turret, freezing cold and carrying a full load of high explosive and incendiary bombs to drop on Berlin.

In less than two hours we were landing at Tegel, one of Berlin's three airports and heading for the waiting coaches. It was a freezing cold day as we visited the Charlottenburg Palace, the Berlin Dome, the Red Town Hall with imposing clock tower, the Reichstag, the Humboldt University, and the impressive Brandenburg Gate. Naturally we had to see the Berlin Wall and the remains of Checkpoint Charlie in the Potsdam Square area with cameras clicking away.

On then to the Kurfurstendamm, one of the city's main shopping streets, to buy a few souvenirs before boarding the coach to return to the airport. A quick visit to the duty free shop and on to the 757 for the return journey. It had been a long day and a hot meal and coffee were very welcome. We had done Berlin and back in around three hours, somewhat quicker than Harry's Lancaster, even though his trip had been one way only.

54. BREMERHAVEN BY MAXI

Testing the Austin Maxi in Germany

Several years ago, when the new Austin Maxi was launched, I was approached by the local dealers, Grimsby Motors, to carry out an extensive road test on the continent. To obtain as much publicity as possible, Tony, the general manager, arranged everything, including sending mayoral greetings to the Bürgermeister of Bremerhaven in Germany. Subsequently we both visited the Town Hall for a photoshoot of the handing over of a gift.

The Maxi by the 'Tor Anglia'

More photographs of the Maxi, gaily bedecked with coloured streamers and balloons, were taken as we left the car showrooms with an escort of Maxis similarly decorated for the port of Immingham to board the Tor Line ferry for

Amsterdam. With the Maxi safely stowed away below, we were introduced to the captain and shown to our quarters, a deluxe suite cabin normally reserved for the ship's officers. A little different from a previous trip I had made in a basic cabin for four people.

The Burgermeister's car with chauffeur

A magnificent meal at the captain's table sustained us during a smooth, uneventful crossing of the North Sea, until breakfast early the following morning. On a bright sunny morning we disembarked at Amsterdam and made our way out of the port with Tony at the wheel and the navigating left in my hands. We took turns at driving, making sure that we recorded the fuel consumption and crossed the border into Germany, heading north east towards our destination,

Bremerhaven. Here we were met at the Rathaus, the German equivalent of our Town Hall, by the mayor of the city and his colleagues. The building was very impressive and after a much needed wash and brush up, we were taken on a tour of the building before being whisked off in the mayoral Mercedes to a restaurant overlooking the harbour.

During a presentation ceremony, I handed over copies of the Lincolnshire Life whilst Tony passed over the gift and Grimsby mayoral greetings. The mayor spoke excellent English (how many of our mayors could speak German?) and he was anxious to know more about our local politics amongst other things. He was surprised to hear that we changed our mayor annually whilst he was in office for 12 years and he was a lawyer by profession. A very substantial meal followed with excellent German wine before being taken to a hotel for our overnight stay. The following day was taken up with a conducted tour of the city before saying our farewells to our hospitable hosts, who wished us well on the rest of our journey.

Heading north on a cold day with a sprinkling of snow, we passed through Schleswig-Holstein and over the border into Denmark. The Maxi was running well and so far no problems, with a petrol consumption of around 45mpg. The inner man was calling for sustenance and lunchtime saw us calling in at a *Kro* for a welcome meal.

Fully refreshed, we had a change of driver and I took over for the remaining miles to Frederikshavn, on the northern tip of Denmark. Here the Maxi was again safely stowed on the ferry to take us over the Kattegat and across to Gothenburg in Sweden. From there we completed our circular trip on the Tor Line ferry back to Immingham. Tony was well satisfied with the overall fuel consumption of the Maxi and was not slow in publicising the fact in the local press and Lincolnshire Life.

Handing over a copy of Lincolnshire Life to the Burgermeister

55. FUENGIROLA

Buying an apartment in Spain

On one of our visits to the Costa del Sol we were wandering around looking in the windows of estate agents just out of curiosity and saw an apartment advertised for sale for £8,000. To our surprise the apartment was in the hotel in which we were staying. From what we heard, some years ago the hotel sold off a number of apartments, which were snapped up by a shrewd Irishman, who then proceeded to sell them individually at a profit. Although we were not at that time considering buying property abroad we went inside to find out more details. The Spaniard, realising that we were English, said he would fetch his partner to deal with us. It was with some amazement that when he came through from his office, I recognised him as being an ex-customer at the Westminster Bank in Grimsby where I had worked.

His name was Ronald Blau and at that time he was a Flight Lieutenant navigator in the RAF and surprisingly he remembered me. This would have been some 30 years later and there was a lot of catching up to do. He invited us into his office for a chat, then we moved on to a local bar for a glass of wine or two. In the course of conversation it turned out that Joan was at school with his brother Lennard, who later worked in the family tailoring business.

He offered to show us the apartment which attracted us and we decided on the spot to buy it. We kept it for about eight years and Ronald organised the cleaning, laundry etc., whilst we rented it out through an agency in England as we could only visit for two weeks each year. The hotel where our apartment was located, Las Palmeras, was not involved in looking after the room and as far as they were concerned it was our private apartment. We could have meals in the restaurant but of course had to pay for them. Initially we used to go down for breakfast and breeze in to the dining room as if we were staying at the hotel as paying guests. However, they eventually realised that we were not official residents and started a check-in system which put a stop to our little game.

We were invited to Ron's house to meet his charming wife, an ex-dancer with the Bluebell Girls. They lived in a delightful villa on the road to Nerja and introduced us to some excellent eating places in the surrounding area.

We went to the resort regularly, got to know the good restaurants in town, and came to regard it as our second home. We had our favourite bars and the owners used to recognise us and remembered what drinks we liked. A favourite restaurant of ours was the Shakespeare, run by an English couple, who cooked an excellent curry, with all the extras such as coconut, mango chutney, nuts and raisins, and a half litre of sangria.

After eight years we sold the apartment and actually made a profit, which is unusual in our history of financial transactions. We would love to go again to see how things have changed and see if our favourite bars and restaurants are still there as it is some years since our last visit.

56. FLORIDA

Share ownership in Weeki Wachee

In one of the Sunday supplements I spotted an article about property in Spain. It was written by Harold Dakin of Sheffield and he said he was disappointed in what Time Share had to offer and he had set up a Share Ownership Scheme. He had advertised and quite quickly had around 50 replies from people who were interested. There was a contact telephone number and I rang him for more details. Apparently the scheme was oversubscribed but he told me that he was going to start a similar scheme in Florida and would contact me later.

This he did, and sent photographs of the bungalow which was being built in Weeki Wachee, about seven miles from the Gulf coast in Hernando County. Bearing in mind that I hadn't even met this fellow, I plunged in head first and said I was interested and sent off a cheque. The bungalow was duly finished and we spent our first holiday there in 1993. There was about a quarter of an acre of land and there were two bedrooms, two bathrooms, garage and all mod cons including of course air conditioning. There was no pool but this was built some four years later. It is about an hour from Tampa airport and two hours from Orlando. The location is just off the Highway 19 on a complex called the Heather, which has tennis courts and a golf course, as well as lakes, one of which is home to an alligator. There were three when we first visited but two were taken away when they grew too big. It is rumoured that when they leave the lake to bask in the sunshine, they have been known to approach the sixth green and have to be persuaded back into the lake with a sharp tap on the snout with a golf club!

9043 Nakoma Way

There are fifteen shareholders and we each take four weeks' holiday on a rota system. Every year we have an AGM in the Birmingham area and agree on a figure for management fee for maintenance for the coming year. We have had some wonderful holidays there and explored most of Florida including a long trek down to Key West – some 500 miles but well worth it. I know that hurricanes are a feature of this part of the world but so far we have been lucky. We have had violent thunderstorms and heavy rain but in the main it has been hot and sunny most times of the year. It may seem a long way to go for a holiday, involving some seven or eight hours flying time, but we found it well worth it, if only for the sunshine, cheap petrol, food and clothes. In addition we made several friends there and came to regard it as our second home.

During this period we visited a time-share presentation at a local hotel in Grimsby just out of curiosity to see what they had to offer. We were quite open with them and told them we already had a shared property in Florida, and after a brief presentation they decided not to waste any more time, and offered us a choice of a prize and said how lucky we were as we had drawn a free trip to the Bahamas. The downside was that the trip started from Fort Lauderdale and we had to find our way there and pay the airfare. This was no problem as we going to Florida anyway, so we took a week in Weeki Wachee then drove down to Fort Lauderdale to board the ship to Freeport. It was about a six hour cruise with entertainment on board. We had decided to upgrade our hotel so it wasn't an entirely free holiday and of course meals were not included. The weather was beautiful and the time passed very quickly, just giving us time to tour the island and visit the casino and other places of interest. Then back to Fort Lauderdale and a long drive back to the 'ranch', where we spent the rest of our holiday. We had taken part in several time-share presentations before, saying no thank you and receiving the usual gifts of wine, spirits and shopping vouchers, but this one was the best we had ever had.

Carol, Joan, and Lindsay with snake

Joan had said that she would like to go to the local Methodist Church so, being an obedient husband, I took her and decided to stay for the service. During the service one couple were renewing their wedding vows on the occasion of their Golden Wedding anniversary. After the service we introduced ourselves and offered our congratulations and in the course of conversation, we found out that they lived on the same complex as we did. With typical American hospitality, we were invited to visit them anytime. We exchanged visits on a regular basis and Betty introduced us to a 'Fuzzy Navel', a potent drink made of vodka, schnapps, a secret ingredient, orange juice and lashings of ice. Her husband Harry just sat back and let her get on with it. His excuse was that she did it so much better. Just as well we didn't have far to drive home. They were known as 'Snowbirds', having decided to leave their home in Kentucky to live their retirement in the warmer climes of Florida. Last year they reluctantly decided to go back home to be near their family as they are both in their early eighties and not in the best of health. We shall miss them.

It was customary after the service to go for breakfast and Betty and Harry introduced us to their friends and it became a regular Sunday outing. There were ten of us and we first visited 'Dad's Diner' then various different restaurants for our eggs, bacon, grits, and pancakes. To have fried eggs and bacon on the same plate as pancakes covered in maple syrup took some getting used to but we managed.

Next door we met another couple who had two homes, one in Florida and one on a small island in the St. Lawrence River. They had apparently built their own log cabin there and transported everything by boat from the mainland. Their son, who owned his own plane, used to visit them and fly over their house, dipping his wings, and then land on the mainland. This was a signal for them to get the boat out and collect him. They were a very talented couple, he was a retired expert in nuclear physics and she was the Director of Art in

America and was an accomplished expert in stained glass windows. We hadn't known them long before we were asked round to celebrate Thanksgiving Day with them and their friends. They are both in their eighties and still very active.

In the area there are so many restaurants and we tried most of them and found it easy to make friends with people sitting nearby. On one occasion, in a Chinese restaurant, we met a couple who owned a construction company and they invited us to look around their luxury housing development. The properties were first class but way out of our financial bracket. This was when I committed an unforgivable crime by forgetting to leave a tip. The waitress rushed outside after me to drop a gentle hint and I paid up. How embarrassing.

We were recommended to visit Glen Lakes, a superb restaurant on a prestigious residential complex with a popular golf course. It was here that we became friendly with a couple, he was American and she was English. They had met way back in World War 2 when he was serving with the US Air Force. They married and eventually settled in Hernando County and we were invited to their home, beautifully furnished and with the obligatory pool. We usually meet up at the Glen Lakes each time we visit.

57. MARDI GRAS AND ALL THAT JAZZ

New Orleans

Putting his paper down and taking another mouthful of gin and tonic, Harry said, "How about taking a trip to New Orleans to see the *Mardi Gras* and listen to some real jazz?"

"Sounds like good idea, when do we go?" said I, lazily turning over to even up my tan.

Harry had seen an ad in the local paper for a three night stay in New Orleans, flying from Tampa, at a very reasonable price. At the time Harry and Kathleen were staying with us at Weeki Wachee near the Gulf Coast of Florida, well away from the razzmatazz of the Magic Kingdom and Disneyland, relaxing in the sunshine in the peaceful area of Hernando County.

Jazz by the river

Bookings were soon made and within a few days the four of us were parking the car at Tampa Airport for the hour long flight to 'The Big Easy', as New Orleans is known. Taking a taxi to our hotel, we were given a history of the city by the talkative taxi driver and a list of places to visit. When we complimented him on his knowledge, he said, "No problem, it's all part of our training." As we were on an early morning flight, we arrived at our hotel in time for breakfast and a full day ahead of us. It is traditional to begin the day with coffee and beignets at the Cafe du Monde where you will see the jazz musicians gathering in nearby Jackson Square together with a sprinkling of fortune tellers.

For a little gentle exercise we meandered along the banks of the Mississippi, listening to the busking musicians doing their thing before visiting the Riverwalk Centre. There are over 100 shops here and many restaurants serving a variety of international foods.

To see at first hand the typical Colonial style Plantation homes and abundant wildlife, we took a tour of the coastal wetlands in Bayou country. The ship's Captain filled us in with a fascinating history of the Cajun heritage and culture and legends of the swamps. In the evening we just had to take a cruise on one of the steamboats on the mighty, muddy Mississippi, where we ate on board and tapped our feet to the rhythms of the resident jazz band.

Although New Orleans has more than its fair share of poverty, a trip on a streetcar to the Garden District will reveal the other side of the coin, where magnificent Victorian style mansions and Plantation Homes can be seen. It is possible to have a tour around the huge, newly renovated Louisiana Super bowl, which boasts no less than four ballrooms and a football field, the home of the renowned New Orleans Saints. Yes, the very same ones who 'go marching in.'

The Mardi Gras parades start two weeks before 'Fat Tuesday', the literal translation of Mardi Gras, and we arrived midway through the celebrations. It is described as a rollicking, raucous and ritualistic legendary holiday with a magical infectious spirit and it is certainly all of those. Entering into the spirit of the parade, we had purchased colourful masks and took our places by the barriers of the main street. After about an hour wait, the first float arrived to loud cheering and shouting from the crowded streets. Soon the traditional cries of "Throw me something mister!" went up and we were showered with coloured beads, plastic beakers, doubloons and trinkets thrown by the gaily dressed occupants of the floats. The procession, including several marching bands, horseback riders and the floats took some two hours to pass and the ever present music and good-natured banter made for an enjoyable, unforgettable occasion. The official carnival colours of purple, green and gold, representing justice, faith and power, were well in evidence on the floats and many of the houses on the parade route.

After the parade we took a walk down the well-known

Bourbon Street, in the French Quarter, which was 'heaving' with hundreds of people in a merry state, happy and good humoured. We pushed our way through, pausing to watch the boys tap-dancing on the pavements and listen to the strains of jazz filtering through the open windows of the cafes. Eventually we reached our destination, Preservation Hall, an old building that had seen better days. However, inside, the atmosphere was magical as we stood at the back of the packed hall, tapping our feet to the strains of Dixieland Jazz and New Orleans blues.

Preservation Hall

Unfortunately we had left before Lundi Gras, or 'Fat Monday', when a riotous occasion takes place at the Spanish Plaza with live entertainment and a fireworks display. At the stroke of midnight on the following night, all festivities come to an end, the streets are cleared, the barriers taken down and the floats and costumes stored for next year.

58. NORFOLK BROADS

Abandon ship!

On our previous holiday in Bournemouth we had met a family from Kent and had become good friends. During conversation on our last day they suggested that we meet again and a few venues were discussed before the idea of a holiday on the Norfolk Broads was put forward. None of us had been before and it seemed a good idea. Little did we know what was in store for us.

As pre-arranged, we met at Wroxham, parked our cars and made our way to the boathouse. Our boat for the week looked huge, but there were ten of us in all, four in our family and six in theirs. We were taken on a tour of inspection and packed away our gear, after deciding who was going to sleep where. Then came the interesting bit when we were shown how to control the monster, start, stop and reverse, and how and where to empty the toilet. Very important. After a short run up-river to show us how everything worked, the boat owner handed it over and said, "It's all yours." It seemed a strange thing to do, to hand over an expensive vessel to someone who had never been on a boat before, but who were we to question it? He seemed quite happy to trust us to bring it back in one piece.

By reason of his seniority, Bob took the first spell at the tiller and away we went – but not very far. We had been informed that we could go downriver first as the tide was still low, but as we passed under the first bridge, there was an ominous scraping sound and we were stuck under the bridge. It took some time pushing and heaving at full throttle in reverse to free the boat. By this time a crowd had gathered on the bridge and a loud cheer went up as we shot away in reverse. What a start and how embarrassing. But we weren't finished yet as we had to turn the boat round to go upstream. This wasn't easy as we found out when we tried to do a three (or four or five) point turn. We managed to hit another boat which was moored at the side but fortunately did no damage.

Strawberries for tea

It was a glorious day, sunny and warm as we chugged away at about five knots, stripped to the waist (well the men were). The girls were in their bikinis and quickly found a place on deck to do some serious sunbathing. Bob and I took it in turns at the helm whilst Joan and Phyllis sorted out the provisions for the week.

The first two days passed without further incident and we were all enjoying our first venture on board. On the third day there was a problem with the battery and as it was an important football match on television in the evening, we pulled into the side and moored up by a small pub. We went inside, ordered drinks, and asked the landlord if we could watch the game on TV. He obviously wasn't a football fan and declined, saying he was there to sell drinks and not entertain customers, the selfish swine. We had to contact the boat owner and tell him where we were and he brought a replacement battery.

It is said that everything happens in threes and the next day we tempted providence by deciding to head for Great Yarmouth on the coast. We had our evening meal and found a place to moor the boat with two or three others. There was a warning about the tidal drop in this area and to make sure that we allowed enough slack to allow for this. We followed instructions and went to bed after a few drinks on deck in the remaining sunshine.

It must have been around one o'clock in the morning when we were awakened by the sound of breaking crockery. Leaping out of the bunk, I noticed that the deck was sloping at an unusual angle and saw a heap of smashed cups and plates on the deck. I went up on deck followed by Bob and we saw that the mooring rope was so tight that it had pulled the boat at an angle and a ledge on the side of the boat was caught under part of the bank. The situation was getting worse so we called, "All hands on deck!" and we managed to get everyone ashore with a struggle. Bob and I tried starting the engine and putting it in reverse to try and free it but it was no good – we were well and truly stuck and the boat was floating at an alarming angle. After a discussion I said I would go across a nearby bridge and find a telephone and contact the fire brigade. I told them the position and waited by the phone box until they arrived. I jumped aboard and directed them to our boat. They didn't waste any time, got out their crowbars and tried to lever the boat from the side. At first they said they may have to saw part of the boat to release it, but we persuaded them against this course of action. As all this was going on, the police arrived, wanting to know what it was all about. They were not amused. The firemen managed to release the boat and told us that we may receive a bill from them, but we never received one. So, it was back on board and to bed, though everyone seemed too excited to sleep. Surprisingly, no one from the other boats had heard a sound and never offered to assist us in our hour of peril. An early breakfast gave us the opportunity to discuss the night's events.

The weather was good and it was very relaxing to cruise along at walking pace, eating, drinking, and enjoying the scenery. Under normal circumstances, a boating holiday on the Norfolk Broads is certainly one to be recommended, but be prepared for the unexpected.

59. CORFU

A stormy voyage with Dimitrios

"Wine, anyone?" asked Demetrios, as he took the cork from a bottle of local 'hooch'. Now this was an invitation which very rarely met with a negative response from the passengers – even though it was only nine o'clock in the morning. We were off the coast of Corfu on a trip round the island in the glorious Mediterranean sunshine.

Demetrios opening the first bottle

It had all begun on the previous day at a local taverna where Joan and I were having lunch. We had finished our meal and had entered into conversation with the only other occupants, two English couples. We had all been invited by the taverna owners to look around their kitchen and asked if we would like to learn some Greek dances. Fuelled by the contents of bottles of Greek wine we attempted dismally to follow the intricate movements. During the lesson a local entered and offered to buy us another bottle of wine. The reason for his generosity was soon revealed when he asked us if we would like a trip on his boat the following day. By this time we were all in mellow mood and arranged to meet him at the harbour, first thing in the morning.

There was just a gentle breeze as we boarded the boat next morning and although we had only met the previous day, we were already good friends. One couple were from Skegness and the other from Ilkley and when the invitation came from Demetrios, the reply was an instant, "Why not?" After the first glass of 'Domestos' was hesitantly tasted, it was agreed that it wasn't so bad after all and the bottle was emptied before we reached our first stop at a beachside taverna for coffee.

This was only our second day in Corfu and life was good as we made our way northward to our next stop for lunch. On returning to the boat after lunching ashore, the weather had deteriorated and ominous black clouds had appeared. Our skipper decided, wisely as it happens, to cut short the trip and return to home base. How right he was, for as headed out to sea, the rumblings of thunder could be heard in the distance, the wind had risen and the sea had become decidedly choppy. None us were particularly good sailors and when Demetrios offered to open another bottle of wine, we declined.

As the sea became rougher and the rain started to fall, we went below whilst the skipper donned oilskins and sou'wester and struggled to keep the boat on a straight course, in the now very rough seas. Not one of us had been at sea in a small boat in stormy seas and we looked nervously through the tiny portholes at the raging sea and wondered if we would make it back to harbour. Unfortunately, the hotel landing stage had been swept away by rough seas and Demetrios bravely managed to find an alternative landing place to drop us off. We were so relieved and I think Demetrios was too as we bade him farewell. This had been the only bad day during our stay and we were happy to spend the rest of our holiday relaxing in the sunshine by the pool.

Joan and bearded friend

60. FRIENDSHIPS

What would we do without them?

We have been very fortunate in that we appear to make friends easily and over the years have met some delightful people on holiday, some of whom we still see regularly or keep in touch by mail or telephone. These friendships we value greatly.

Most of us have been on holiday and met up with people with whom they became friendly and on the last day have said, "Please keep in touch." One couple we met in Corfu, Brian and Joyce, did keep in touch and they lived in Ilkley where they owned a milk round. Unfortunately a heart attack forced him to sell his business and during his recuperation period he carried on with his hobby of painting. His landscapes were much admired and he found that he had no difficulty in selling them. He opened an art gallery in Skipton when they moved to Coniston-with-Kilnsey and continued to make a living from his paintings.

We used to exchange visits every year until his wife died suddenly. We went to the funeral and afterwards Brian asked us to keep in touch. Subsequently he invited us over for a weekend and it was an emotional meeting. Once the tears had gone he said in his typical down-to-earth Yorkshire dialect, "Right, you are in your usual room, I told you not to bring any bedding as I'm a dab hand with the washer but I can't cook." So off to the local pub we went for a meal and a pint of Yorkshire bitter. Their home was an old grey stone house, beautifully decorated and tastefully enhanced by the artistic talents of Joyce, just across the road from the village church. The situation was a walker's paradise, as a few steps out of the house past the church and up the hill and you were on the moors.

As the weather wasn't too good, he took us to see his new summer house, where we spent the afternoon helping him to drink a three litre box of French wine (not all at once). He had bought a Mexican bread oven which looked like a pregnant chimney pot and we took it in turns to feed it with logs to keep the fire going. It was rather a sad, nostalgic afternoon but once the wine had taken its effect Brian cheered up and we went once again for a pub meal to meet friends of his. To be on the safe side, he left his car at the pub and we all came home in his friend's car. They left at midnight, Joan went to bed, and Brian and I stayed up yarning until two in the morning.

It had been a good weekend and he appeared to be coping in his own way. He was not an ambitious man and told me that if he could sell a couple of paintings a week, he would be quite happy. From time to time he has a meeting with his accountant and in his forthright manner says to him, "Never mind the complicated details – all I want to know is, have I got more coming in than going out!"

***

In the fifties when the children were young, we used to visit Bournemouth for our holidays. The hotel we stayed at was owned by a couple from Lincolnshire and as it was a small family hotel, we got to know some of the residents who came year after year. One such couple were Betty and Fred from St. Albans, who came with their son Andrew and daughter Linda. Their children were about the same age as ours and we became friendly to the extent of booking for the following year each time we went. We exchanged addresses and regularly used to visit each other's homes as well as having a holiday together in Menorca. Fred had this strange habit of carrying on his person a piece of coal, a cork, and a piece of string and found it embarrassing going through customs at the airport when he had to empty his pockets. He celebrated his 80th birthday in 2002 at the home of Linda, who was then living in Doncaster and we were invited to celebrate with the family. Sadly he died in 2003 and we still visit Betty once a year on his birthday.

***

During my banking career I was transferred from Grimsby to St. Martins, Leicester. It was here that I met Peter Lowe, a friendly soul and a bit of a character. Each year the bank was represented at the Leicestershire Show and Peter was there as cashier in the mobile bank. In addition to looking after the customers financial requirements, he and his assistant were required to offer hospitality by supplying drinks. On one occasion Peter had helped the customers in consuming drinks and apparently had more than his share, resulting in his attempt to drive his car through the turnstiles. How he managed to get away with it I don't know.

We became friends and when I resigned from the bank he had retired to Derbyshire and we used to visit him and his wife, Sheila. They lived in a delightful house called 'Hatters Castle' in the village of Lea, where Peter liked to make his own wine. He kept it in a converted pig-sty and invited me for a tasting. The wine was delicious and some two hours later we returned to the house in a happy state to some stern words from our wives. They later moved to a listed *'olde worlde'* house with the name 'Cottage-in-the-Meadow' with a fair amount of land and Peter decided to buy a horse. He had been in the cavalry during the war and he was regularly seen at the local village pub, where he used to tether his nag to a post outside the pub before going in for a pint.

Sadly he died, as a result of war wounds, some years ago, but we still visit Sheila, who now lives at a house with another unusual name 'The Old Creamery' in the village of South Wingfield.

***

When I was at Leicester branch of the bank I went on relief to Belgrave branch, where I met Malcolm Flint, who had a natural flair for telling jokes. We were on the counter together and he kept me in fits of laughter. He was some twelve years younger than I was, but we had a lot in common. After I resigned, Malcolm was transferred to Lincoln and we arranged to meet. Subsequently he retired through ill health and went to live at Long Bennington, near Newark. Sadly he suffered from cancer, but was in remission, though he never complained. He also used to sing in a male voice choir but had to give up on doctor's orders. A great lover of music, he started to play the cornet and visited a band in nearby Newark, where he was allowed to sit in at rehearsals. A keen motorist, he is a member of the Advanced Drivers organisation. We still meet once or twice a year with him and his wife Jennifer.

***

When Joan was in the Silhouettes Operatic Society, she met Frank Jobson, who later on joined the Orpheus Male Voice Choir. Through various social functions we came into contact with Frank and his wife Kitty and became friends. When Kitty died I shall never forget when the choir sang 'Sunset Poem' at her funeral and Frank joined the choir to sing with them. That must have taken some doing. Some time afterwards I asked Frank round for a coffee and a chat. This became a regular practice and on these occasions we discussed the choir, the state of the country, and generally put the world to rights, in our opinion anyway. Some years later he confided to me that he was considering leaving Cleethorpes and going down to Herne Bay in Kent, where his daughter and son-in-law lived. It was a difficult decision, but in the end he went and bought a bungalow near his daughter. Sad to say, but he was taken ill and died in April 2005 and his funeral took place in Cleethorpes, when the choir, of which he was an Honorary Life Member, sang a moving farewell.

***

You read about neighbours from hell, but we are very fortunate as we have friendly neighbours on each side. John and Pam, whose wedding anniversary coincides with ours, on one side, and Noel and Jean on the other. During holidays, we each look after each other's houses, which gives us peace of mind whilst away. Whilst I was in hospital last year for four and a half weeks, Noel cut my grass and made sure my bins were emptied. Jean was good company for Joan and their efforts were much appreciated. Noel, being a Welshman, is naturally a rugby follower and does his best to introduce me to the intricacies of the game, but I prefer the game with a proper round ball. When we went to our place in Florida we invited Noel and Jean to join us for a couple of weeks and managed to sink a litre or two of delicious Californian wine. When we go out for a meal in the UK, we are very fortunate as Jean doesn't drink, so we don't have a driving problem. Although they are some ten years younger than us, we get on very well, even though they speak a strange language.

***

When I was in Rotary I persuaded my Bank Manager, Harry Stephenson, to join the Immingham Club. We became friendly and in due course exchanged visits to each other's homes. In fact when I was in the bank, I worked alongside his brother, Len, who died in a cycling accident. Harry's wife Kathleen was a nurse in Canada for many years before returning to the UK and they too have been out to Florida to visit us. We also had a five day break with them in Amsterdam, where we visited places of interest, which included the red light district (with our wives of course). Various one-day flights to European capitals were advertised and Berlin seemed a popular choice, so the four of us were up at the crack of dawn to catch the flight from Humberside Airport. It was a long, tiring day but well worth it. In the future they are contemplating moving to Yorkshire, where they have several ex-banking friends. We shall miss them when they go.

***

My old mate Bryan Hammond sat next to me in the choir and he used to come round to our house where the two of us tried to learn our music, with Joan knocking out the notes. To refresh our parched throats, I offered some of my homemade lager to Bryan and it certainly had the desired effect. I knew then that it was a good brew, which wasn't always the case. He was divorced from his wife, who left him, taking their daughter and was naturally not feeling too happy with life. He eventually got engaged to Sheila, also divorced with a daughter, and they were married in 1978. Bryan used to come with me on the driving weekend at the Mintex testing ground and we had some hilarious times, both on and off the track.

***

During one of our holidays in Cyprus we stayed in Paphos and always went out for our evening meal to one of the many restaurants. Sitting next to us was an English couple, and Joan being chatty, engaged them in conversation. They came from Blackpool and introduced themselves as Jo and Gordon. They are both keen golfers and he is a gifted organist and presented me with a cassette of some of his recordings. They were staying in an apartment and after the meal we invited them back to our hotel for a drink. This became a habit and a friendship started. I had hired a car and the four of us toured the island and nearly ran out of fuel on a lonely road on the way to the Monastery. We had to turn back and just managed to find a petrol station in time. As we normally do, we exchanged addresses and visited each other's homes, and are still in touch.

***

On the occasion of one of the 9 Squadron reunions we met a couple from Wollaston. Don was an ex-Flight Engineer on Lancasters and he and his wife Jean had come by caravan and after the dinner and speeches we went to see them off.

The drinks had loosened our tongues and we had become friends overnight, resulting in an invitation to their home for a weekend. Don was a retired builder and local councillor and had built his own house. It was beautiful home with an acre of land on the outskirts of Wollaston. This was the beginning of another lasting friendship and to this day we exchange visits.

***

In our home town we have a regular eightsome with three other couples and take it in turns to host a dinner party. Don is a farmer at Beelsby and he and his wife Rosalie usually leave the party at ten o'clock as he says it is past his bedtime! Peter was in car sales and is now retired, and his wife Gill sings in a local choir. Peter is teetotal but Gill likes her wine. Joy and Derek are originally from South Africa, but have settled in Grimsby. Each year Joy returns to their homeland, but Derek stays at home – why, we can't imagine. He is very fit and gets up around 6am for a run in all weathers. We always stock up on red wine when he is coming as he is a great wine lover. This arrangement has been going on for a few years and hopefully it will continue.

***

Brian and Meriel used to live in Grimsby, where he was a member of the Orpheus Male Voice Choir. He was transferred to Stockport by his company and eventually resigned and bought a property nearby to sell paintings and make his own frames. Following this, they bought a gift shop with house attached in the Lake District. As Managing Director of the company he had worked for, he had become disenchanted with the hassle of union problems and found more pleasure out of the 'rat race' in running his own business. We have exchanged visits, but now they have moved to France and bought a house there. They visited the UK a short time ago and called to see us and we now have an invitation to stay with them in France. They have settled in well and Brian speaks the language fluently, though Meriel is having a few problems.

***

I was not a regular church-goer but Joan went every Sunday and had become friendly with Kath, also a regular. In due course I met her husband, Des, who had been a rear gunner in Wellingtons in the Middle East in WW2. He was quite a character and brewed his own beer. He used to ask me round whenever a new brew was ready and boy, was it strong! A couple of halves and we were well away, much to Kath's dismay. We visited each other's homes and became Scrabble addicts, Kath usually finishing as winner. Sadly both of them are no longer with us and died within a year of each other.

***

When we were married in 1951, two of our guests were Colin and Christine. Joan had known Christine for many years and when they were married four weeks later, we were invited to their wedding. This friendship goes back a long way and Colin, who is a year older than me, suffered a heart attack some years ago. Fortunately he recovered and has learned to live within his limitations. They have three boys, all married and living away, but their daughter is still living in the area. We exchange visits and go out for meals together from time to time.

61. SILVER, RUBY, AND GOLD

Anniversary celebrations

The year 1976 was the occasion to celebrate our Silver Wedding Anniversary. We decided to have a bit of a do and booked a room at the Winter Gardens in Cleethorpes. The question was, who to invite. In the end we invited family and close friends to lunch in the restaurant and later, an open invitation to the Orpheus Choir, which at that time was around 65 strong. Drinks and a buffet were provided for the lads and we celebrated appropriately.

Our Ruby Wedding Anniversary took place at the Ross Club (now, alas, gone) where the Orpheus had organised their popular Christmas Cracker parties for several years. All the choir, plus family and friends were invited and the ever popular Leo Solomon entertained us on the piano. The bar was open and a delicious buffet was put on by the catering staff. Another day to remember!

In the first year of the new century, on the occasion of our Golden Wedding, we had a decision to make. Do we, as some of our friends have done, book a cruise and get away from it all, or do we celebrate at home with all our family and friends? We chose the latter as we felt that it wouldn't be the same, just the two of us toasting each other with a glass of bubbly. So, back to the same venue as our Silver for an afternoon meal and celebration with family and close friends, around 50 in all. Although it was late September, it was a beautiful day, just what we had prayed for, with glorious sunshine and a first class view of the shipping on the River Humber. A happy occasion watching the grandchildren enjoying themselves, background music of our favourite items and the inevitable speech by me. This was one of the very few occasions that I had delivered a speech and of course I had it prepared days beforehand. I am not one for witty, off the cuff speeches, so this was done from a typewritten script. No idiot board for me. We were particularly pleased to have with us Christine and Colin, who had married one month later in the same year as us, and still remain friends. Here's to the next time!

Cutting the 'Golden' cake

62. HOME SWEET HOMES

Where we have lived

With stars in our eyes and love in our hearts, we moved into our first home at 24 Compton Drive in 1951. It was a semi-detached house with a small garden and no garage, but to us it was heaven. It was within walking distance of town and not too far away from my in-laws, who had been of great assistance in many ways, including finance. Lindsay was born there in 1955 and a year later we moved to Park Avenue.

Number 61 Park Avenue was an older house not far from Barratts recreation ground, where we used to play tennis. We paid £1,600 for the house and spent around £200 on a new damp course and redecorating. The garden was larger than our previous house and there was a garage. The bottom of the garden overlooked allotments and we befriended one of the holders with a view to receiving fresh garden produce. It was here that Carol was born in 1959 and two years later I was transferred to the Westminster Bank at Leicester.

The city of Leicester was quite different from Grimsby and I spent some 12 weeks in a hotel before finding a suitable house. In 1962 we moved into 215 Glenfield Road, a four bedroom semi-detached house on a dual carriageway. It was a busy road and some way from the bank but it was an ideal family home with a large garden. During this period I was transferred to Loughborough branch, some 15-20 miles away. Eventually I grew tired of commuting every day at my own expense and resigned in 1967 to return to Grimsby.

Back in Grimsby we bought a house at 82 Weelsby Road, only two doors away from my mother-in-law! It was a fairly old house, built in 1912, with high ceilings and proper skirting boards, but a lovely home. There was a small garage which I extended and just a small garden with greenhouse, which suited Joan. The only problem with living on a main road, as in Leicester, was reversing out into the traffic at rush hours.

Lindsay was married from 82 and in 1981 we made a joint move with Joan's mother and father to Cleethorpes.

Over the border into Cleethorpes we moved into 24 Denby Drive into a four bedroom detached house with a large garden and double garage. Joan and I lived upstairs and her mother and father lived downstairs. Carol slept downstairs and we all dined together at meal times and it worked very well. Carol was married from 24 and Joan's mother and father both died whilst we were there. It was a large house for the two of us but we got on so well with our neighbours that we were reluctant to move. As I write this we are still here and no doubt we shall be spending our final years here. Our first house was 24 and our last will be 24, unless of course we are in a home!

63. WHAT NEXT?

A summing up and look into the future

It is now 2005 and I am approaching my 80th birthday. My father died when he was 63, my brother was 57 when he died, and some of my relatives passed away around the 60 mark, so I have the feeling that I am living on borrowed time. Only the male side of the family have been affected by this phenomenon as my mother lived to her early seventies. I look upon it as a bonus to have survived so long. I suffered a mild stroke in 2002 and went to hospital for a *carotid endarterectomy* to clear my arteries and now take six tablets per day to keep the blood flowing. Apart from that and the usual effects of ageing I am fortunate enough to be reasonably healthy. I am a member of the Humberston Country Club, where I go twice a week for a workout in the gym followed by a Jacuzzi and swim in the pool. Twice a week I play badminton at Scartho and the College with younger players, except for one who is 83 and still going strong!

Since I started writing this, I was diagnosed as having bowel cancer and had major surgery in October 2004 for a colostomy. My way of life has changed, but with the support of Joan and family and friends, I have come to terms with it. I walk each day to build up my strength and hopefully will be playing badminton again and returning to the gym.

We are both members of the Wine Circle, where activities include barbecues, visits to wine growing areas and of course wine tasting evenings. Last year we joined the U3A (University of the Third Age) where Joan attends gardening sessions and I settled on something less energetic, 'Armchair Travel.' Just to fill in the spare time I recently joined

PROBUS (Professional and Businessmen), an organisation which meets once a month for a meal, a speaker, and conversation with like-minded retired people in a sociable atmosphere. In addition, I joined the NatWest Pensioners Association and we meet, with wives, three or four times a year at the Golf Hotel in Woodhall Spa for a meal, a glass or two of wine and a speaker.

My wife Joan, who was a Shorthand and Typing teacher at the Cleethorpes College of Commerce, was instrumental in introducing me to the joys of singing as she came from a musical family. She used to sing duets with a friend as well as the occasional solo part in the operatic society. She also sang with Lindsay and Carol on special occasions. Her interests did not coincide with mine (apart from our love of travel, eating out and drinking wine) as she played bowls, is a member of the local flower club, goes line dancing and is secretary of a church fellowship group.

Both my daughters followed in my footsteps and originally worked in banks. Lindsay now works part-time at a solicitor's office and Carol is employed full time as a School Secretary. The grandchildren are at that difficult teenage stage and the dreaded O levels are not so far away. My only granddaughter Rebecca is into gymnastics and horse-riding and at the moment has ambitions to be a doctor. She has also taken a modelling course with a view to emulating one of the top models and earning thousands of pounds a day! She also is a dreamer like me! Her brother Adam is also into gymnastics as well as squash, tennis, and football.

Carol's son James, played football for a time until he became hooked on Kart racing and has collected several trophies already. Could he be another Michael Schumacher and achieve one of my ambitions? His brother Matthew is into sports and plays football in a local team with Adam, as well as having regular tennis coaching sessions.

Both our daughters chose their partners well, Lindsay

marrying Steve, a Senior Controls Engineer with BP. His second love is squash and he became club champion whilst he was in Abu Dhabi in the oil business. Carol married Nick, a Company Director and a keen cyclist and karting enthusiast. He is also an excellent cook.

Steve sadly lost his father some years ago but his mother is still in the area and takes over the duty of child minding from time to time. Nick's mother and father are caravan and walking enthusiasts and spend a lot of time away from home. We get on well with them and count them among our friends, exchanging visits.

THE FAMILY IN 2005
Back: Steve, Lindsay, James, Nick
Front: Adam, Rebecca, Carol, Matthew

Sadly, our close family connections will suffer in July 2005, when our daughter Lindsay, together with Rebecca and Adam, will be joining her husband Steve in Moscow, where he has taken a new appointment with BP. This is for two years, with an option to extend to five years, but at least they are not at the other side of the world and we hope to visit them there.

64. MOSCOW

Since I signed off in 2005, life has changed considerably. After the departure of Steve, Lindsay and family to Moscow, we were invited to join them for a holiday. Our only visit to the Russian capital was some years ago when we spent a night there on the way to Abu Dhabi in the United Arab Emirates. This time we spent two weeks there staying with our family. A quick flight of 40 minutes to Schipol from Humberside and then three hours by KLM to Moscow. Their rented home has five bedrooms, all ensuite, and a double garage. The house is located some 16 miles to the north of the city in Rosinka, an International Residential complex with security guards patrolling constantly. There is a private lake, a school, mini-market, restaurant, and sports centre.

With a population of around 10 million, the city is home to more billionaires than in any other city. Vladimir Putin was elected President of the Russian Federation in 2000.

The grandchildren both went to the Anglo-American School and were taken each day by one of the Russian drivers allocated to each BP employee. The two drivers also took my son-in-law to work and my daughter shopping and took all of us out for a meal in the evening. The driving habits were most unusual as they thought nothing of driving on tram lines or pavements!!

There are no postmen or milk deliveries. Post is collected from a delivery point, milk is purchased in the local shop, and a free copy of the Moscow Times is available at the mini-market or Sports Centre.

The following year our other daughter, husband and two boys went with us, all ten of us in the five bedroom house.

What a fantastic time we had but little did we know that it would be the last time that all the family would be together on holiday.

65. CARIBBEAN CRUISE

We had only been on one cruise, which was some time ago around the Mediterranean when the girls were teenagers, so I was tempted to go on my own on a Caribbean Cruise. Unfortunately single persons are penalised by the Single Supplement, which added quite a lot to the cost and my double room could have slept three people comfortably.

In 2009 I flew from Doncaster to Santo Domingo in the Dominican Republic and boarded the Royal Caribbean ship 'Vision of the Seas'. The two week trip included calls at Antigua, St. Kitts, Barbados, St. Lucia, St. Maarten, Margarita Island, Venezuela, Aruba.

Tables were allocated for dinner and my companions were two American couples and a couple from Kent. The Americans were not particularly bothered about dressing up and mostly wore casual attire. At the end of the voyage I was invited by one of the American couples to visit them on their farm in Pennsylvania but never made it.

On day four I was stricken by some type of virus and had to visit the Medical Officer. I had a fever and high temperature and my blood pressure was very low, so I was put on a drip for an hour. At eleven o'clock I returned to my cabin laden with medication and antibiotics, with strict instructions to stay in my cabin for 48 hours. I had to ring for food which was brought promptly and missed seeing one of the ports of call. However, I received a letter from the Welfare Officer, wishing me a speedy recovery and including a voucher for £750 to go towards another cruise with the company. Not a bad offer for two days' sickness! This was used the next year on a Mediterranean cruise.

66. FAMILY HOLIDAY

In 2014 I was invited to join the family for a holiday on the Algarve. It was great to be with all the family, except for Joannie, and it could well be the last time when we are all together. Although the grandchildren are in their twenties, they gave up their usual holiday with their friends of similar age to come with their parents. An excellent time was had by all apart from my fall climbing out of the Jacuzzi, when I badly bruised my thigh. My daughters looked after me and arranged for a wheelchair at the airport.

67. FAREWELL MY LOVE

On April 24 2007, my dear wife Joannie died. She suffered a severe stroke and was paralysed down her right side and was unable to take nourishment. She was in hospital for four weeks and we visited her every day, hoping for an improvement, but sadly it was not to be. The family flew home from Moscow for the funeral and it was gratifying to see a full church. The Orpheus Male Voice Choir were present and sang 'Sunset Poem' and 'My love is like a red, red rose.'

After the funeral I was invited to Moscow to be with my family and surprisingly it was one of the hottest months they had had for many years, with temperatures of 30 degrees Celsius.

So, at the ripe old age of 82, I was on my own and realised just how much I missed her. No welcoming voice when I returned home and only myself to talk to. The pain is still there and I realise that I have to make a new life for myself.

ADDENDUM

Since the death of my wife in April 24th 2007 I have taken solo holidays to Paphos, Lanzarote, Madeira and Turkey. Enjoyable though they were, it was never the same as having a loved one by your side. In addition we had a family holiday in the Algarve in 2014 involving the whole family and I guess that this will be the last holiday together as a family. The grandchildren are in their twenties and in the future will be going their own way and I am very fortunate that they were happy enough to share their time with a doddery old man!!

I count my blessings.

The years have passed by and it is now August 2015, ten years since I first starting writing this story of my life. Since my wife's death eight years ago , I have lived on my own in a house far too big for me, but with a lot of happy memories. My daughters Lindsay and Carol and families, have been very supportive, as have my friends and neighbours, during a difficult period of coming to terms of life without a loved one.

After a health problem last Christmas, when I spent seven weeks at my daughter Lindsay's home, I have come to the conclusion that I must take steps to either downsize to a flat or move everything downstairs on one level. As I get on well with my neighbours I have decided to stay until the grim reaper calls from above – or below. I realise that I must be realistic as in September this year I shall reach the ripe old age of ninety.

My daughters and their husbands are settled and in good health and my four grandchildren are all in employment. Boy friends and girl friends have appeared on the scene and who knows, marriage and great grandchildren may be on the way in due course. I may not have achieved any of my ambitions but I have had 55 years of happy marriage with my dear wife and consider myself a very fortunate and contented man.

19302877R00129

Printed in Great Britain
by Amazon